SLAYING
YOUR
GOLIATHS

HOW GOD CAN HELP

SLAYING
YOUR
GOLIATHS

HOW GOD CAN HELP

JOHN OHMER

FORWARD MOVEMENT
CINCINNATI, OHIO

DEDICATION

ACKNOWLEDGMENTS

Thanks to those who have formed me and allowed me to minister among them: William Placher and Eric Dean of Wabash College, the faculty and students of Virginia Theological Seminary, the Rev. Andrew Merrow and the people of St. Mary's, Arlington, Virginia, the people of St. James', Leesburg, Virginia, and now the astonishingly gracious and welcoming people of The Falls Church Episcopal. Thanks to Scott Gunn and Richelle Thompson of Forward Movement for believing in this project and bringing it to fruition. Thanks to Bill and Lucinda Michel for loaning me their Deep Creek cabin for uninterrupted writing time. Thanks to the Rev. Jeunee Godsey and the Rev. Mary Davila for their help in writing the discussion questions, and to the Rev. Cathy Tibbetts, Julie Huang Tucker, Nina Bacas, the Rev. Michael Hinson, Kathy Thomas, Jim Councilor, Terri Katon, the Rev. Rosemari Sullivan, and the Rev. Jean Milliken and now the Rev. Kelly Moughty, and my other good colleagues at The Falls Church. Thanks be to God for the Diocese of Virginia's belief in, and fight for, The Falls Church Episcopal. Even though I don't know them, thanks to Glennon Doyle Melton and Rachel Held Evans for spiritual writing inspiration. Thanks to my Jesuit spiritual directors and to counselor John Goll for grounding and regrounding me over the years. Thanks—twenty-seven years of daily thanks—to my wife, Mary, for her belief, patience, and love. Most of all, thanks be to God for putting our children, Graham, Will, and Elizabeth, plus all these people, in my wonderful life. And to God be the sole glory.

TABLE OF CONTENTS

PREFACE

It's fair to ask: "Why another book on David and Goliath?"

The answer to that question is contained within the hope-filled promise of this book: *How God can help you, like David, overcome seemingly impossible odds.*

Take a look at each word and phrase:

How. This David and Goliath book comes from a working pastor—a parish priest—and it is intended to be a practical, how-to book. For the last twenty years, my chief responsibility and joy has been to help make God and the Bible real to people and applicable to their lives and work. I've sought to do that through sermons, Bible studies, retreats, and everyday conversations.

In late 2012, I left my job as the rector (senior pastor) of a relatively large, well-established church in order to accept a call to become the rector of a much smaller congregation called The Falls Church Episcopal, located just outside of Washington, DC, in Virginia. I joined this faith community—at the time consisting of about eighty people on a Sunday morning—shortly after they were allowed to return to their massive property in the midst of what would be a six-year divisive legal battle that was litigated all the way to the United States Supreme Court (and only finally resolved in 2014).

Together, we have wrestled with a lot of "how" questions: How are we going to heal the divisions of the past several years? How are we going to grow membership and fill our buildings? And even: How are we going fix the leaking roof and pay the bills?

Against this backdrop, the David and Goliath story has taken on fresh meaning. Because underneath a lot of our "how" questions is a deeper question that almost everyone asks at some point or another: How am I going to make it? And underneath that question is a deeper question yet: Is there a God "up there" who will help me? And if so, how?

This book pulls together practical lessons that I've learned in my most recent struggle in helping to regrow a congregation—as well as principles I've discovered over the course of twenty years of parish ministry.

I'm confident that if you take the principles of this book seriously and put them into practice, you will learn how...

God can help you. While this is a how-to book, unlike a lot of others in that genre, this is not a self-help book. That's because the David and Goliath story, as originally told and as explored here, is a spiritual story. It is a story told by people of faith to people of faith. The hero of this story is not David, but God.

Yet God is an unusual hero, because God does not barge into the story—David's or yours—but waits to be invited. God does not kick down the door to our hearts but stands at the door and knocks.

It is up to you to invite God in. Once invited, however, God can help you. Indeed, God will help you...

like David. David worshiped the same God that Moses did. When Moses encounters God at the burning bush and asks what God's name is, God says "I am the God of your father, the God of Abraham, the God of Isaac, and the God of Jacob" (Exodus 3:6).

In other words, God is not some remote, distant, indifferent god, but a God who gets involved in the lives of real-life, specific, named people.

What do Abraham, Isaac, Jacob, David, and you have in common? They were, and you are, real living people whom God stands ready to help…

overcome seemingly impossible odds. It is often said that God helps those who help themselves. But that statement is found nowhere in the Bible. In fact, the Bible consistently teaches that the exact opposite is true: God is constantly helping those who cannot help themselves. God helps the helpless.

In fact you might say God is a God of the helpless, not to mention the hapless and the hopeless. Those are the people whom God helps the most. This is good news.

In other words, God tends to favor the underdog. And nowhere is that tendency more powerfully told than in the David and Goliath story.

Better news is that David's story can be our story. Because whether it is bullies in school, mounting personal debt, health problems, or professional challenges, at some point, we all face "Goliaths" in our lives: seemingly insurmountable odds that wear us down or threaten to destroy us.

The even better news is that no matter how insurmountable the odds—however large the giants—they only seem insurmountable. Their size is a matter of perspective. Measured against our size, our abilities, our resources, they can be intimidating. Measured against God's size, God's abilities, and God's resources, however, these challenges can be overcome.

So, why this book? To show how the same God who helped David slay his Goliath stands ready to help you overcome your Goliath.

John Ohmer
Rector, The Falls Church Episcopal

INTRODUCTION

Like many people—like you, perhaps—I thought for most of my life that David and Goliath was a children's Bible story. I thought it had a simple plot: David, a brave, young shepherd-boy, slays, with his trusty slingshot, the heavily armored giant named Goliath. And I thought it had a simple point: Sometimes, against all odds, the little guy wins.

But recently I discovered the story in a whole new way. In particular, the last few years, as I struggled with personal and professional ministry challenges, I found myself drawn back to this ancient story, as if it were an old and trusted friend. And each time I revisited the story, it offered me new insight and new encouragement.

In rereading the story, I have discovered something primal about it. Far from being a simple children's story, it addresses deep emotional yearnings of adulthood; far from having a simple plot, it is full of complex and nuanced storytelling; and far from having just one point, the story has many things to teach us about a variety of modern, real-life issues.

For example, when we read about Goliath's pre-battle taunts, we learn a lot about psychological intimidation and bullying. David's encounters with his older brothers show us that while twisted and broken family dynamics are nothing new, sibling rivalries and petty jealousies can reveal insecurities in even the most confident people. When we see how David handles those who question his ability to take on Goliath, we learn a lot about faith in God and where calm confidence comes from. And when we see David reject Saul's armor and go down to the river to pick out his five smooth stones, we realize we are reading a masterful metaphor about the importance of rejecting ideas or customs that don't fit us so that we can be free to use our God-given gifts.

Most of all and best of all, when we read the David and Goliath story as a spiritual story, it addresses a deep spiritual hunger within us: our longing to know if we are alone in our struggles.

The answer, as we'll discover together in the following chapters, is an emphatic no. We are not alone in our struggles, because the same God who cared for David cares for us.

The story of David and Goliath is found in 1 Samuel 17. (You can read it in the Appendix).We will spend the rest of the book looking further into those ideas. But first, let's make sure we understand some of David and Goliath's backstory.

CHAPTER 1

BACKSTORY

●

The David and Goliath story takes place at an unusual time in Israel's history—during its first kingship. Up until this point in Israel's history, from the time of their liberation from slavery in Egypt until King Saul, judges and prophets had ruled over Israel, not kings. That was the way God wanted it because God wanted Israel to think of God as its only sovereign and protector, not some earthly king. But the Israelites kept insisting, "We are determined to have a king over us, so that we also may be like other nations, and that our king may govern us and go out before us and fight our battles." (1 Samuel 8:19-20)

Eventually, God allows Israel to have what they want, and the people anoint Saul as their first king. But God remains unhappy with the idea of an earthly kingship in general and with King Saul in particular.

Finally, God gets so fed up with Saul that God decides to reject him as king and anoint someone else in his place. To implement this plan, God tells the prophet Samuel to go to the city of Bethlehem, to a man named Jesse who has eight sons, and once there, to follow the instructions that God will give him.

Here is how the story of the anointing of the new king goes (you can read the full accounting in 1 Samuel 16):

Jesse's first son, Eliab, is brought before the prophet Samuel. Eliab is tall and handsome. More importantly, he is the oldest of the eight sons, and so everyone thinks that he is going to be anointed king. But God tells Samuel it's not Eliab who should be king: "I have rejected him," God says to Samuel, "for the LORD does not see as mortals see; they look on the outward appearance, but the LORD looks on the heart." So Jesse's next-oldest son, Abinadab, is brought to Samuel, but he, too, is rejected. The same thing happens with Jesse's third-oldest son, Shammah.

Jesse then makes his next four sons go before Samuel, one at a time. But it's the same story: "The LORD has not chosen any of these."

Finally, Samuel asks Jesse, "Are all your sons here?"

And that is when we first learn about David.

"There remains yet the youngest," Jesse says, "but he is keeping the sheep."

"Bring him," Samuel says.

When David is brought inside, God tells Samuel, "Rise and anoint him; for this is the one."

Then Samuel takes the horn of oil and anoints David in the presence of his brothers. (Keep this in mind for later in the story!)

The next thing that happens is "the spirit of the Lord came mightily upon David from that day forward," and at the same time, "the spirit of the LORD departed from Saul."

So God's spirit—the divine favor or protection of God—flows into young David and out of King Saul—leaving Saul technically the king but now spirit-less. Favor-less. Unprotected. Actually, it's worse than that: Not only does God's good and holy spirit depart from King Saul, but also an evil spirit, a foul spirit, a distressing, agitating, unhappy, and paranoid spirit, takes its place.

A bit later, back home in the palace, King Saul's servants notice this evil spirit tormenting the king. Because music and musical instruments were considered things that could tame or banish evil spirits, Saul's servants ask the king for permission to find someone who can play the lyre for him, to comfort him.

When King Saul agrees, guess who is suggested. "A son of Jesse the Bethlehemite." David himself! So King Saul summons David to serve him. David acts as the king's armor-bearer, and over time earns the king's trust and affection and even love by playing the lyre for Saul whenever Saul feels under attack by the evil spirit. And sure enough, each time David plays the lyre, the evil spirit goes away and King Saul feels relief.

So that's our backstory. That is where the story of David and Goliath begins. Do you see why this backstory is important? David will eventually re-emerge as one who is willing to battle the Philistine giant Goliath. And eventually, after Saul's death, David will become king—and one of the most well-known figures in the Old Testament. (This is the same David who will achieve fame as a military hero and shame as one who succumbs to temptation when he sees Bathsheba bathing; it is the same David who is credited for composing many of the psalms. And this is the David that the gospels of Matthew and Luke list as a direct ancestor of Jesus.)

But before all this, we know:

✔ God did not want the Israelites to put their trust in an earthly king because it would lead them to believe that protection and security come from the king's weapons and resources and not from God.

✔ God has rejected Israel's first king, King Saul, and anointed David as his successor.

✔ David is a surprising choice to be the king's successor: He is only a shepherd boy, and he is the youngest and therefore least likely of his eight brothers to be selected.

✔ David is a controversial choice to be the king's successor because he was anointed king in the presence of his older brothers, breeding resentment.

✔ David, presumably having kept his anointing a secret, is now working for King Saul, comforting him over the loss of the very God-spirit that David now possesses.

A CHURCH IN NEED

The Falls Church Episcopal has a rich history going all the way back to the 1730s. For most of its history, it had been moderate in size and a full and cheerful part of the wider church of the Diocese of Virginia and The Episcopal Church. But in the mid-to-late 1980s, it went through a period of massive numerical growth, in its heyday having about 3,000 baptized members and drawing an average Sunday attendance of about 2,000. During this time, its leadership began expressing increasingly strident opposition to the wider Episcopal Church, particularly around the issue of full inclusion of gays and lesbians in all aspects of church life and its policy of allowing women to become bishops.

These differences of opinion led to a formal church split in 2006, with the vast majority voting to leave The Episcopal Church and only a hundred or so members voting to stay within it. Shortly after the vote, three longtime lay leaders of church—Bill Goodrich, Bill Fetsch, and Harry Hudson—met to decide what to do next. They made a decision that any course of action had to follow from praying and worshiping together. Shortly after, about thirty people gathered for worship in the living room of Bill and Robin Fetsch as the "continuing congregation" of The Falls Church Episcopal.

Meanwhile, the "departing" congregants (now calling themselves The Falls Church Anglican) attempted to make a legal case that they were entitled to remain in the possession of the buildings and grounds and that the property belonged to the local parish, not to the diocese or wider Episcopal Church. While other area congregations that chose to leave The Episcopal Church made similar arguments, they settled at some point or another with the Diocese of Virginia. (For example, at least one Anglican congregation now rents church property back from the diocese.)

In 2012, the Virginia Supreme Court unanimously ruled against The Falls Church Anglican and in favor of the Diocese of Virginia. That decision required the departing group of parishioners to leave the property they had attempted to claim as their own. (They now occupy office and worship space nearby.) The Virginia Supreme Court decision also allowed the group of "continuing Falls Church Episcopalians" to return to the property.

Unfortunately, even after the Virginia Supreme Court decision, the leadership of The Falls Church Anglican chose to continue litigating the matter, which meant the case dragged on for several more years. The US Supreme Court declined to hear the case in 2014, which officially let the Virginia Supreme Court decision stand, finally ending the legal battle.

The Falls Church Episcopal still had major challenges, even though they were back in the building and the lawsuit was settled. The congregation had about eighty or so people attending Sunday worship services in the fall of 2012. Sure, they had outgrown the parishioners' living room and even their space at a Presbyterian church, but now, there was plenty of space to fill— and expenses to meet—in the newly reclaimed church building.

FOR FURTHER REFLECTION:

1. How does knowing his humble beginnings inform your understanding of David's story throughout the Bible? How does this backstory influence your reading and understanding of the psalms? Does it change your view of the story of David and Goliath? How?

2. Before you face your Goliaths, why is it important to know and understand the backstory? How might this context shape your next steps?

CHAPTER 2

WHEN WE'RE STUCK, GIANTS THAT *SEEM* BIG *ARE* BIG

●●

If you are familiar with the David and Goliath story, you probably think it begins with a battle scene. But it actually begins with what is supposed to be a battle scene.

Two armies—the Israelite army and the Philistine army—are facing each other about fourteen miles west of Bethlehem. A few miles away is a fortress called Azekah, which the Israelite army is intent on protecting against a Philistine attack. If the Philistine army is going to attack Azekah, they must first cross through the Valley of Elah, a large *wadi*—an Arabic word for a river channel or ravine that is usually dry, except during the rainy season.

Picture the scene in your mind: Two armies are facing each other, preparing to fight, gathered on opposite hillsides (or mountainsides) with the Valley of Elah, a dry riverbed valley, in between them.

And the two armies are only preparing to fight; they are not actually fighting. Each day they go through the motions of getting ready to fight: forming into lines, probably pounding their spears or rattling their swords, shouting, rallying. But no one is actually fighting. Day after day, this goes on.

Why? Well, remember they are on opposite hillsides. They can look across the Valley of Elah at the other army, but to get to the other army they would first have to run down their hillside, enter the lower ground of the dry riverbed, and then charge back uphill to where the other army was stationed.

You don't have to be a military expert to know that under those circumstances, it would be foolish—more than foolish, it would be mass suicide—to be the first ones to charge. As any modern-day nation with a good air force knows, it's a huge advantage to hold the higher ground, to fight from above. In the low-tech battles of that day, soldiers didn't have guns and mostly fought in hand-to-hand combat with swords and spears. Think about it. Would you rather throw a spear uphill at the person you are fighting, or downhill? Would you rather run uphill to attack someone or have gravity on your side, running downhill?

These seasoned armies full of experienced soldiers knew all about those military advantages. So while it may seem odd for two armies to gather for battle and go through the motions of fighting every day but with no actual fighting, you can see why there's a stand-off, with neither army willing to go first.

As the story of David and Goliath begins in 1 Samuel 17, this deadly game of chicken has been going on for a long time. Both sides are stuck. But one side—Israel's army—is more stuck. That's because each day for forty days, every morning and every evening, one soldier from the Philistine army comes out and shouts at Israel's army.

He is described as a champion, and his name is Goliath.

Goliath is an expert and seasoned soldier. And his height is described as six cubits and a span—almost ten feet tall—or, in what is said to be a more reliable text,[1] four cubits and a span, which would make him about 6 feet, 9 inches tall.

Goliath has a helmet of bronze on his head, and he's armed with a coat of mail—overlapping metal scales, like those of a fish—that weighed five thousand shekels of bronze (somewhere around 100 pounds). He's wearing bronze shin guards. A javelin or scimitar is in between his shoulders.

He's carrying a spear as large as a weaver's beam—think of a fence post. The tip is made of iron, a metal much harder than bronze, which most armor was made of in those days. The spear tip alone weighs six hundred shekels, or about fifteen pounds.

GIANT STRESS

I joined the "continuing congregation" of The Falls Church Episcopal in 2012, shortly after the Virginia Supreme Court had ruled in their favor and they were allowed to return to their church building. This small group returned not only to their historic, colonial-era sanctuary that seats over 300, but also to the other main sanctuary that was built in the early 1990s during the church's rapid growth period. The main sanctuary seats well over 900 people.

So as I joined this congregation of 80 to 100, we had some giants to face. One was how to take care of and then grow back into these sprawling facilities that had been built for a mega-church. This brought giant financial pressure: Even though the continuing congregation was growing and generous, annual expenses

---

[1]Harper-Collins Study Bible, NRSV, Wayne A. Meeks, General Editor, note on 1 Samuel 17:4 says, "The Masoretic Text's 'six cubits and a span' make the Philistine champion almost 10 feet tall. According to the Septuagint and a scroll from Qumran (4QSama), which probably preserve a superior reading here, he was 'four cubits and a span,' or about 6 feet, 9 inches tall—a true giant but not a fairy-tale monster."

were running about $700,000, in part because of deferred maintenance; annual giving was about $200,000. We survived those first few years because of assistance from the Diocese of Virginia and neighboring Episcopal churches such as St. Mary's, Arlington. They invested in us, believed in us, and worked with us because they believed in our potential. But we all knew their financial commitments could not last forever.

At the same time, there was the stress of the continuing legal battle. Would the US Supreme Court hear the case? If so, would it rule in our favor, or was there some possibility we would have to move out again? Then there was the giant stress of having come through a major church split: Many families were literally split between The Falls Church Anglican and The Falls Church Episcopal. And finally, there was the challenge of managing change: the welcome-but-difficult changes that come when a church grows from a small, intimate congregation where everyone knows each other by name to what would soon become a larger congregation with several full-time clergy and multiple staff.

Now granted, I have not been in a lot of hand-to-hand fights in my life, but the idea of an armor-piercing spearhead the weight of a bowling ball coming at me is not something I'd look forward to.

Here is a question that many people ask at this point: Are all these descriptions an exaggeration? Are they a kind of biblical hyperbole that makes for good storytelling? Was Goliath really between 6 feet, 9 inches and 10 feet tall? Did he really wear so much heavy armor and carry such large weapons?

The way I would answer that question is to ask another question: What difference does it make?

If the purpose of the David and Goliath story is to convey lessons about how God helps David—and us—slay our Goliath, then are the actual measurements of one's giant important?

If you are stuck, paralyzed in fear, facing seemingly insurmountable odds, and there is a giant facing you, if something or some situation weighs heavily on your heart and takes up a lot of space in your brain and seems huge to you, then do the exact facts and figures really matter all that much?

The exact number of feet and inches of Goliath's size? The precise number of pounds and ounces of his armor? Thinking about those things is like thinking about the exact percentage of a compounding interest rate when we are faced with crushing debt and trying to decide whether to make a payment on an overdue credit card or buy diapers. It is like thinking about exactly what questions will be asked on a final exam when we're facing a stack of unstudied books, or the precise combined side effects of radiation and medications when we have just received news of an inoperable cancer.

In such times, in such circumstances, exact details, exact facts and figures don't really matter, because when we're stuck, giants that seem to be big ARE big.

FOR FURTHER REFLECTION:

1. Pause at this point in your reading and ask yourself: What is my Goliath? What is the giant in my life right now? Your giant could be personal, something you, family, or friends are struggling with. It could be professional, some challenge facing your business or faith community or school. Name it. Write it down.

2. If you are facing several Goliaths, name them all. Then ask yourself, which one seems the biggest? Keep in mind that reality and the cold, hard facts and figures don't really matter here, because whatever Goliath seems the biggest to you is the biggest to you. Which one looms the largest? Which is second?

—∿∿—

As I've spoken to a number of groups about this story and asked them to do this exercise, I've come up with a list of many common Goliaths that people face. Glancing through that list (after you have made your own) may help you. [See Appendix.]

The exercise of naming your Goliath may produce some stress. But if you look at what other people have listed as their giants, then the overall exercise can be a stress reliever. You can see that the fears you felt were uniquely yours are actually shared by many others.

CHAPTER 3

A GIANT'S SECRET WEAPON: WORDS

Naming your Goliath can be a breathtaking exercise: It can knock the wind (the spirit) out of you, leaving you feeling overwhelmed. Before we move on to the good news (I promise it's coming), let's take a closer look at that demoralizing dynamic so we can understand it better.

Specifically, let's take a closer look at the backstory that has been going on for forty days: Goliath waging what we would now call psychological warfare against Israel's army. Every day, morning and night for well over a month, this giant soldier steps out in front of his army and shouts across the valley at the army of Israel. He always says the same thing: "Why have you come out to draw up for battle? Am I not a Philistine, and are you not servants of Saul?"

Notice something here: Long before the David and Goliath story has anything to do with a physical fight, long before David even shows up on the scene, something important is going on between Goliath and the Israelite army that can teach us a valuable lesson about the giants we face in life.

First, Goliath's words, "Are you not servants of Saul?", contain a deliberate insult to Israel's army. Remember from the backstory that

Saul is Israel's very first king. The Israelites had been around for a long time, but it wasn't until this exact time in their history that they had an earthly king. They knew God was not happy with their insistence on having a king. In fact, "God grieved" over having made Saul king partly because of the way Saul behaved after being made king, but mostly because God knew that the people Israel would shift from trusting in God to trusting in their king.

Here's the critical point: God wanted the people Israel to always think of God and God alone as king. God wanted the Israelites to remember that it was God who delivered them out of slavery and oppression in Egypt; it was God who provided security and protection from their enemies. Therefore it was God in whom they should trust, not in themselves, their military might, or in any human ruler.

But for a variety of political and military reasons, plus the desire to be like other nations, they wanted a king. They begged for a king. And despite God's warnings, they got one: King Saul. And so now here is Goliath, referring to the Israelite soldiers as "servants of Saul." Not servants of God, as they had long believed themselves to be, but servants of Saul!

I believe this is a deliberate insult. The Israelites in general, and soldiers in particular, had to be sensitive about this. For generations, they had thought of themselves as servants of God, believing that they were protected by God. But here is Goliath, referring to them as servants of a mere human being, implying they are now just like every other nation.

You see what is going on here? Goliath, like anyone engaged in warfare, is trying to demoralize his enemy. Day after day, he tries to get under the skin of the rank-and-file Israelite soldiers. He tries to plant seeds of doubt in their hearts and minds.

He wants the soldiers to wonder if they had made a mistake in making Saul their king. Maybe Goliath was right, and they had become just another earthly kingdom, just another army. Had they lost their divine protection?

Does Goliath's strategy work? Well, there is a fascinating little detail at this point in the story: We are told that "when Saul and all Israel heard these words of the Philistine, they were dismayed and greatly afraid."

We are accustomed to thinking that Israel's soldiers were terrified of Goliath's size. And they probably were—as we have seen, he is huge.

But that's not what the story itself says. They are not just intimidated by Goliath's size, they are terrified at hearing his words. There is something about his language—what Goliath is saying—that is making them afraid.

The same is true about modern-day Goliaths who come against us: Part of what makes them so imposing, so scary, is that they mess with our minds. They dis-courage us—and to be dis-couraged means that our courage has been taken away.

> Before there is ever an actual fight, the Goliaths we face in life attack our heart, our will, our sense of well-being, trying to demoralize us through fear-inducing rhetoric.

Sometimes this rhetoric—the intimidating words we hear—comes from the giant we are facing. Sometimes there really is a bully who sneers insults across the playground or through the Internet. Some people suffer verbal abuse from a parent or spouse who says horrible things like "You're worthless" or "You'll never amount to anything." Sometimes the car needs a new transmission at the exact same time you have taken a pay cut, and the bills on the dining room table scream overdue.

Those external words, those giants, are difficult and scary. But in some ways, those external words are easier to fight off because they come from outside of us, and we can work with others to find ways to ignore them or counter them with healthier, more supportive messages and strategies.

The harder words to fight, I have found, are those that come from within us. They are the gremlins or tapeloops of self-doubt inside our own heads. I am referring to those times we question our own value or worth with subtle but potentially debilitating words: We are thinking of applying to our dream school or for a dream job, and there is a voice saying, "Who do you think you are?" We are getting ready to deliver a speech or make a presentation, and there's a voice that says, "You're unprepared; you're going to make a fool of yourself and be exposed as a fraud and a failure." You are thinking about starting a new diet or exercise routine, and there is a voice that says, "It's never worked before; you're not beautiful or attractive, so why bother?"

What causes these words to have so much power? What causes them to seem so real and believable even when objectively, there isn't much basis in fact for them?

I think at least part of the answer comes from psychologist and bestselling author Brené Brown.

In her book, *The Gifts of Imperfection*, Brown reassures us that feelings of inadequacy or self-doubt are quite common. In fact, she writes that most people see ourselves as "never _____ (fill in the blank) enough." We see ourselves as never thin enough, never smart enough, never successful enough. The list is endless, and constantly changing.

Behind all those voices, Brown writes, is a message of never good enough. And what drives the "never _____ enough" voice, Brown says, is our culture's overall scarcity mentality; Brown quotes another author, Lynne Twist:

> For me, and for many of us, our first waking thought of the day is "I didn't get enough sleep." The next one is "I don't have enough time." Whether true or not, that thought of not enough occurs to us automatically before we even think to question or examine it. We spend most of the hours and the days of our lives hearing, explaining, complaining, or worrying about what we don't have enough of. …
>
> Before we even sit up in bed, before our feet touch the floor, we're already inadequate, already behind, already losing, already lacking something. And by the time we go to bed at night, our minds are racing with a litany of what we didn't get, or didn't get done, that day…This internal condition of scarcity, this mindset of scarcity, lives at the very heart of our jealousies, our greed, our prejudice, and our arguments with life.

If Brown is correct that our "never enough" thoughts are rooted in our wider culture's scarcity mentality, you can see how the giants we face in life seize on these thoughts. Just as Goliath wanted David and the rest of the Israelite army to feel small and ill-equipped, the giant problems we face in life try to do the same thing. If they can make us feel unprepared or inadequate, then they have defeated us even before we start to fight. We have allowed ourselves to feel that we cannot measure up.

Goliath's intention—and the intention of the giants we face—is to diminish us.

Just look at the roots of the word diminish. They are from the Latin *diminue*, which means to speak disparagingly or to lessen someone verbally, and from *minutia*, which means smallness. So to diminish someone is to use disparaging words to make them feel small. If a giant can diminish us, the battle is won without ever being fought. If we feel diminished, we are filled with a sense of resignation. And resignation almost always leads to inaction, borne out of a sense of "Why bother?"

So for forty days, the words of Goliath have King Saul and the Israelite army stuck, frozen, cowering in fear. Feeling diminished, resigned to their situation, no one is able to move; no one is willing to take any action. No one, that is, until David appears on the scene.

Recall that David has not joined his older brothers in the army. He has been going back and forth between being home with his father, tending sheep, and serving Saul as a musician. His father, however, gets curious about his older sons and how they are doing, so he sends their younger brother David to take food and other provisions to them, to check in on them, and to bring back a report. David arrives and starts wandering around Israel's camp looking for his brothers.

One day he overhears Goliath's threats, and not having been there the last forty days, not having been subjected to the psychological warfare, and therefore having an entirely different perspective than the soldiers standing around, David offers to step up and fight Goliath.

But he doesn't get to fight him right away, because, as we will see in the next chapter, when you offer to step up and slay a Goliath, people will grumble.

FOR FURTHER REFLECTION:

A giant's secret weapons are words. If words can do the work of diminishing us and make us unwilling to take action or do anything about a situation we are in, the giant has won the fight before it ever begins.

1. Reflect on and write down some examples in your own life when the diminishing words came from an exterior source. Name some examples of diminishing words that came from the interior. Share with others if you feel comfortable. Which seemed the most believable to you? Which was the most effective at diminishing you? Which ones are recurring?

2. What are your most frequent "I'm not ____ enough" thoughts? Make a list.

   ✔ Which ones seem the loudest?

   ✔ Which feelings of scarcity or inadequacy seem to be the most limiting in your life?

   ✔ Which ones are you most easily able to ignore or push past? What has helped you do so?

   ✔ Look back at your list of "not _____ enoughs" and compose affirmations to counteract the loudest of the giant's words. "I am _____ enough to _____." Or "I have enough _____ to _____."

   For example, "I have several longtime friends." or "I have enough confidence to speak to a room full of people."

3. Sometimes seemingly harmless expressions such as "Oh well," "*Que sera sera*," "Whatever!" and "It is what it is," are said in a well-intentioned or even healthy way—as if to say, "I'm not going to sweat it" or "I think I'm going to make

peace with this situation." Many times, however, something more insidious is implied. Often these expressions are said in the exact same tone as "Forget about it!" and stem from a diminished self-image or with a heavy tone of resignation. Think about times you tend to use these expressions. Are they signs of a healthy sense of peace or are you resigning yourself to something you should be fighting? Can you think of examples? How might you check yourself to see if you are giving up a fight before it starts due to voices of inadequacy or diminished self-image?

CHAPTER 4

IF YOU OFFER TO STEP UP AND SLAY A GOLIATH, PEOPLE WILL GRUMBLE

Author and spiritual leader Marianne Williamson wrote, "Our deepest fear is not that we are inadequate. Our deepest fear is that we are powerful beyond measure…as we let our own light shine, we unconsciously give other people permission to do the same. As we are liberated from our own fear, our presence automatically liberates others."[2]

I like this quote very much and have it printed out where I can read it as often as possible. And while I am sure Marianne Williamson addresses the downsides of letting our own light shine elsewhere in her writings and lectures, I am afraid this quote skips over an important point that I would like to address in this chapter:

> Sometimes when we let our light shine and we are liberated from our fear, our light threatens others, and our fearlessness angers them.

When David offers to step up and slay Goliath, eventually his light and fearlessness liberates others. But first, there is grumbling and opposition and even attempts at sabotage.

---

2 *A Return to Love: Reflections on the Principles of "A Course in Miracles,"* Marianne Williamson, 1992.

That grumbling, opposition, and threat of sabotage are not reasons to quit. But lest we get discouraged, we need to be aware of the dynamic so vividly described in the David and Goliath story—that when you offer to step up and slay a Goliath, people will grumble.

As the story picks back up, King Saul and the Israelite army are still stuck, staring across the valley of Elah, cowering in fear upon seeing Goliath's size and feeling diminished upon hearing Goliath's words.

Then Goliath moves in for the kill, or at least the threat of a kill: He challenges anyone in the Israelite army to a man-to-man, winner-take-all combat:

> Choose a man for yourselves, and let him come down to me. If he is able to fight with me and kill me, then we will be your subjects; but if I prevail against him and kill him, then you shall be our servants and serve us.

Goliath is offering a man-to-man fight to the death. If someone from the Israelite army takes Goliath up on the offer, and that soldier wins, then the whole army of Israel wins. But what happens if Goliath wins the hand-to-hand combat? Israel's soldiers become slaves of the Philistines, one of their most dreaded enemies. The stakes couldn't be higher.

After issuing this challenge, Goliath goes on to say, "Today I defy the ranks of Israel! Give me a man, that we may fight together."

Enter David.

David, scripture makes a point to remind us, is the youngest son of Jesse, and Jesse has a total of eight sons, the three oldest of whom "had followed Saul to war."

The story then repeats the detail that David's three eldest brothers, Eliab, Abinidab, and Shammah, went off to war. It also reminds us that David is not in the army but rather spending his time going back and forth from serving Saul to tending his father's sheep in Bethlehem. When a Bible story mentions something one time, it is usually important. When a Bible story repeats something, it is almost always a deliberate attempt to get the reader's attention, as if to say, "HEY! SOMETHING IMPORTANT IS GOING ON HERE!"

What is important to remember at this point in the story? At the time the prophet Samuel came to Jesse's house in Bethlehem, each of the oldest brothers probably thought he was the one who should have been anointed as king. But they all had to stand there and watch David, their youngest and therefore least likely brother, get selected and anointed instead. Now here they are, out on the battle lines serving as common soldiers in Saul's army, while David gets to go back and forth between playing music for King Saul and tending sheep for their father back home. As you read the story, you can just feel the resentment and tension between David and his brothers— even before David shows up on the scene.

David arrives at the army's encampment at the direction of his father. Jesse had asked David to take some provisions—grain, bread, and cheese—to his brothers and their commander and to find out how they are doing.

This is another thing to remember: David was not sent by military commanders with weapons to the battle line in order to fight. He was sent by a worried father with groceries in order to check in on his brothers!

David gets up early in the morning, puts his sheep in the care of another shepherd, and loads up the provisions. He gets to the army encampment just as the soldiers are doing their daily ritual: lining up in battle formation and moving toward the battle lines. He sees the Israelite and Philistine armies facing each other and shouting, just as they have for the previous forty days.

David leaves the food with the keeper of supplies, runs out to the battle lines, and checks on his brothers. As he is talking with his brothers, once again, Goliath comes out from the Philistine battle lines. And once again, Goliath shouts his usual taunts. *Why do you come out and line up for battle? Am I not a Philistine and are you not servants of Saul? Today I defy the armies of Israel! Pick a man to fight me!*

And once again when the Israelites see Goliath and hear his words, they run away from him in great fear. Except this time, David is here. This time, David overhears Goliath's words.

And that is not the only thing David overhears. All the Israelite army is abuzz with talk about promises that King Saul has made to anyone who defeats Goliath. *Have you seen how this man keeps coming out and decrying Israel? The king has promised a huge reward to anyone who kills him. Not only that, but whoever kills him gets the king's own daughter in marriage. And he and his whole family would be exempt from all taxes in Israel!*

Lots of cash…marry into royalty…no taxes for life. Sweet deal! But no one has taken King Saul up on the offer. David hears about all the good things for the person who kills Goliath. He asks, "What shall be done for the man who kills this Philistine, and takes away the reproach from Israel?" And then David adds another critical question: "For who is this uncircumcised Philistine that he should defy the armies of the living God?"

The people answer David's questions the same way, telling him whoever kills Goliath will get a huge monetary reward, the king's daughter in marriage, and no taxes for life.

But that is information David already knew! So why would David ask the first part of his question? Why get the soldiers to repeat what will be done for whoever successfully challenges Goliath?

Because David's question is really a rhetorical one. It is more of a statement than a question. And it is a statement that tells us a lot about David's natural leadership ability.

David is shifting, or at least attempting to shift, the focus of the paralyzed-in-fear soldiers from something that is intimidating and diminishing them (Goliath) to something that is encouraging and upbuilding (the reward for defeating Goliath).

And when David asks the second part of his question, notice how David makes two very important points.

The first is in how David refers to Goliath: He makes no mention of his size. He says nothing about his demoralizing words.

No, the first thing that David mentions about Goliath is that he is "an uncircumcised Philistine." Why is this so important? Well, recall that the rite of circumcision goes all the way back in Israel's history to Abraham; it is the sign of God's special and unique covenant with, or promise to, the Israelites. What David believes—but others at the battle lines seem to have forgotten—is that they, the circumcised, are in a special covenantal relationship with God, and by implication, those like Goliath, who are the uncircumcised, are outside that special relationship.

And here is the critical thing: With circumcision, with that special covenantal relationship, comes assurances of divine protection. God has your back. Without circumcision, outside that special covenantal relationship, comes zero divine protection: You are on your own.

God's promise, God's covenant, is foremost in David's mind. So David couldn't care less how large this Goliath is or what he is saying. From David's perspective, Goliath is merely an uncircumcised Philistine, someone who lacks what he has, which is divine protection.

The second point that David makes in his question is that Goliath is defying "the armies of the living God."

Remember that Goliath was using psychological warfare against Israel by referring to them as servants of Saul, implying they were just ordinary soldiers under the orders of an ordinary king, fighting for an ordinary nation. For forty days, they have been diminished by Goliath's taunts, but up until now, when David asks his question and makes these points, no one has reminded them of their true identity: They are soldiers in the army of the living God.

So David is not just asking a question. He is implying, out loud, that anyone who is outside the protection of God and stupid enough to challenge the army of the living God is bound to fail.

By asking this question, David introduces a new mindset and takes a firm stance. And that helps explain what happens next: When David's oldest brother Eliab hears David ask his question, there is an ugly, vicious, and highly personal confrontation. Eliab questions David's very presence near the battlefield. Then he insults David personally. And finally, ironically, he questions David's courage.

In an angry tone—in fact, the New International Version translation of the Bible says Eliab "burned with anger"—Eliab confronts David, asking, "Why have you come down?"

In context, that's an intimidating question. "Why have you come down?" means a lot more than, "Hey, I'm curious, what's the reason you're here?" It means something more like, "What the hell are you doing here?" Said with a sneer, in anger, it means, "Who the hell do you think you are?"

Remember, David was not a soldier. He was standing, presumably in civilian shepherd clothes, amidst a bunch of armored military men. Eliab's question is also a statement. It means, "You don't belong here: this isn't a place for you." It even means, "You should have stayed home, because this is a place for real men, not you."

The story doesn't tell us, but I wonder if Eliab's question is getting under David's skin. Here is his oldest brother, the heir, the wise one, the soldier, up in David's face. After all, Eliab has been serving in Saul's army, going through military training, sleeping in tents, drilling and preparing for war, while David has been playing music for Saul and tending sheep. *Do I have what it takes?* David could well be wondering. *Am I only a musician, a shepherd? After all, my father only sent me to bring bread and cheese. Who am I to be asking these questions, implying that these soldiers have forgotten who they are? Do I belong here? What was I thinking?*

COURAGE IS CONTAGIOUS ————————————

I am no stranger to self-doubt. Before coming to Falls Church, I had served for fourteen years at a congregation that grew steadily and was free from any major controversies. We had challenges, but none were large enough to shake my confidence that I could help grow a church. We were well-established, financially secure, and had every reason to be confident in our future. But when I accepted the call to serve at The Falls Church Episcopal, I found myself in new territory. No longer was I the leader of a congregation of nearly 600 on a Sunday with annual giving of over $1 million. Now I was leading a congregation of fewer than 100 on Sundays with annual giving of just over $200,000—but with bills over $700,000. We had not one but two large church sanctuaries, dozens of empty offices, and we were in the midst of a long and uncertain legal battle.

As I commuted the thirty miles back and forth from my hometown in Leesburg to the city of Falls Church, I could hear the intimidating words of the external and internal giants I was facing. "Why did I come here?" I would ask myself. "Even with help from the diocese and the wider church, how can they—how can we—possibly make it? What do you think you're doing here? Sure, you exude all this confidence when you're out in front of people, but who do you think you are? Shouldn't they have called someone else? You don't belong here—this isn't a place for you. You should have stayed home; this is a place, this is a calling for a real minister, a real pastor, not you."

In those early days of my new call, I kept coming back to David and Goliath, particularly this point in the story. Because far from being simply a confrontation between David and his brothers, this part of the story seemed to offer a study in the dynamics of demoralization and a lesson in why discouragement—and courage—can be contagious.

But that is only the start of Eliab's grumbling against David: After questioning his very presence at the battlefield, he insults him personally. "With whom have you left those few sheep in the wilderness?" Eliab asks, and goes on to say, "I know your presumption and the evil of your heart; for you have come down just to see the battle."

Wow.

That is a lot of hostility, a lot of anger. Let's unpack some of it.

First of all, when Eliab questions with whom David left the few sheep in the wilderness, he is reminding David that he is only a shepherd. Recall that shepherds in David's day and age were not highly thought of. Today, we tend to romanticize shepherds, especially around the time of Christmas pageants. In keeping with a long tradition (going all the way back to Saint Francis of Assisi), every church I have served has a sweet manger scene during the Christmas pageant. The shepherds—my children have played the part—wear their cute little bathrobes and sing their songs and stand just right, shepherding their even cuter cotton-ball sheep.

But 2,000 years ago in rural Palestine, shepherds were at the bottom of the economic and social scale. Back then, when you thought of shepherds, cute would not be the word that came to mind. Filthy, maybe. Smelly, probably. Shepherds worked for what we would consider minimum wage, doing work no one else wanted to do. In fact, shepherds were considered so dishonest that Sanhedrin texts (ancient manuscripts of the day) list herdsmen—shepherds—among those ineligible to be judges or even witnesses in court. So when Eliab reminds David that he is a shepherd, he is deliberately insulting or trying to diminish David.

Eliab then turns insult into injury by getting even more personal, calling him conceited and wicked. Again: Wow. David is conceited? Evil? And he is accused of being there only to see the battle. But what battle? As we have seen, there has been no battle—only a forty-day standoff with the Israelite army cowering in fear. Such out-of-proportion accusations often come when we have struck a nerve with others.

Let's take a closer look at what would cause Eliab to say such things, to make such accusations. First, recall that Eliab had been present and passed over when the prophet Samuel had come to his hometown to anoint a new king. He had to stand there and watch his younger brother—his youngest brother—be chosen over him and his other brothers.

The Bible doesn't tell us what happened after Samuel left Jesse's home and before Eliab and the older brothers joined Saul's army, but presumably there was a time when David and his brothers all shared the same household. This was a time when David had just been anointed king over all of Israel. Can you imagine the tension in that household? Remember the biblical story of another youngest, favored son, Joseph? He was given a coat of many colors by his father, which provoked the jealousy of his older brothers to the point that they tried to kill him. Was a similar story repeating itself in Jesse's home? Did the brothers tease David about his kingship? Or did David flaunt his new status, telling them to bow down to him because one day he would be king?

Here is another thing to remember: David has gone to the front lines of what is supposed to be a battle and started asking questions that remind people of things they had forgotten—that they have God's protection and Goliath does not, and that as soldiers in the Israelite army, they are not Saul's army but actually the army of the Living God.

But what is the reaction? Applause? A surge of courage in the rank and file? Pats on his back and hearty thanks from his brothers?

No. Quite the contrary. When David steps up, the first thing he hears is grumbling. And that grumbling doesn't come from strangers.

It's a sad fact of life that grumbling, undermining, and attacks often come not from strangers but from those

> closest to us: family members, colleagues, and friends. And precisely because they are closest to us, we are more vulnerable to what they say. Their attacks and accusations hurt us more than those coming from strangers.

Eliab and his brothers and the rest of Saul's army have been cowering in fear for at least forty days. Goliath has been insulting and taunting them and their character. No doubt Eliab has felt diminished. He has lost his courage. He has forgotten who he is—and whose he is.

There hasn't been a battle to watch, and Eliab and all the other soldiers know it. Then one day, along comes snotty little David, full of boldness and courage.

Because David has not been there every day with the other soldiers, he stands in stark contrast to the others. Demoralization is often a group dynamic. Discouragement and fear can be contagious, spreading like the disease—dis-ease—that they are. It often takes an outsider to give us perspective or remind us of what we have forgotten. When David shows up, much to the annoyance of his soldier-brothers, he is fresh to the scene, able to see clearly and speak prophetically.

This is part of the reason that newcomers are critical, not only to churches but also to all organizations that seek to grow and thrive. Whether newcomers in a church, first-year students in a college, rookies on a sports team, an understudy in acting, or an entry-level hire in the business world, new arrivals tend to bring new perspectives.

It is the tendency of old-timers, the establishment in each of those arenas, to say, "This is done that way." Each time this happens, for better and for worse, a culture is perpetuated, a tradition is passed on, a habit is reinforced. It is the rare old-timer or veteran who asks the question, "Why is this done that way?"

For example: When our son was a junior in high school and in the middle of applying to colleges, I suggested we start scheduling on-campus visits. That is, after all, what I did when I was his age, and that's what a lot of other parents and kids were doing. I took for granted that college visits were part of the application process, almost as a rite of passage.

However, our son didn't seem to take much interest in scheduling the visits, so one day I asked him, "Don't you think we should go visit the colleges you've applied to?"

He said, "No, I think we should only visit the colleges that accept me. What's the point in visiting the ones that don't?"

I stood there, stunned. Maybe he had a point. Maybe he had a fresh perspective—a new way of thinking about a process I took for granted and had never really thought through.

That is not to say that old-timers and the traditions they tend to uphold and protect are not valuable—or that fresh perspectives are always better. For example, I would not want my airline pilot to climb in the cockpit and toss aside the pre-flight checklist as a cumbersome tradition that stifled his or her creativity. As someone who serves in The Episcopal Church, I appreciate the comfort of tradition and even predictability people experience week by week as they participate in familiar worship customs and recite old prayers and hymns. And as a parent who loves our family tradition of going out to a Christmas tree farm to cut down our tree each year and drinking hot apple cider afterwards, I would be the first to howl in protest if someone said, "Hey Dad, let's buy an artificial tree from the store and drink frozen slushies instead."

If a custom, tradition, or mentality is serving a good purpose, if it is life-giving and enjoyable, if it is still working, accomplishing that which it is supposed to accomplish, then we should have the wisdom to preserve it. Change for the sake of change is not wise, nor should we welcome it.

But we also need to recognize the value of outsiders and newcomers and the fresh perspectives they can bring. So often in our lives, if someone speaks with David-like language of boldness and courage, their words stand in painful contrast and as an unwelcome reminder to those who have lost their boldness and courage.

> If you offer to step up and slay a Goliath, people will grumble, because vision, courage, and perspective can be threatening to those who have resigned themselves to fear and narrow points of view.

When you are confronted by critics, the key is to have a David-like reaction to efforts at sabotage: Turn to God as your source of courage and hope. Measure the giant you are facing against God's size and not your own. In other words: Don't tell God how big your problems are; tell your problems how big your God is.

FOR FURTHER REFLECTION:

1. Using thoughts from this chapter and drawing on your own experiences, why do you think people grumble when someone steps up to slay a Goliath?

2. Can you name times when you have felt threatened or angry, or ready to grumble when someone else has let their light or their fearlessness shine in the face of a giant? Can you describe why you felt that way? How and when have you met opposition when trying to do the brave thing?

3. In Mark 3:21, while crowds thronged around Jesus because of his healing, exorcisms, and teaching, Jesus' family, "went out to restrain him, for people were saying, 'He has gone out of his mind.'" Compare this to the interaction between David and his oldest brother, Eliab. To what extent do you think the negative reaction of those closest to us is meant to protect us (out of concern), to reprimand us (out of anger), or to protect the reputation of the family or group (out of self-interest)?

4. David's questions reframe the conflict with the Philistines in the context of serving in the army of the Lord. Can you reflect on a time when you were able to see a difficult situation with a new, more accurate lens? How did it change how you approached the giant?

5. It is common to dismiss, actively oppose, or question the motivation behind the ideas or action plans of those closest to us. When might it be appropriate to be wary? Under what circumstances might you want to give those persons and their ideas more credence?

6. Do you agree that a newcomer's perspective is good for an organization? Describe a time when a fresh lens helped you or an organization.

CHAPTER 5

DON'T TELL GOD HOW BIG YOUR PROBLEMS ARE. TELL YOUR PROBLEMS HOW BIG YOUR GOD IS.

David Heifetz reminds us in *Leadership Without Easy Answers* that it is important for a leader to "get up on the balcony"—to get above the crowd in order to gain (and keep) perspective.

People of faith, like David, get up on the balcony by measuring their problems against God's size, not their own.

There is a popular expression that makes this point: Don't tell God how big your problems are. Tell your problems how big your God is.

You see, one thing makes David different from the rest of Israel. One thing makes him confident he can defeat the giant. And the same thing that makes David different can make you different, as you step up to slay your Goliath.

And that is David's perspective.

It's what Glennon Doyle Melton, the author of a popular blog, "Momastery," calls the importance of wearing new "perspectacles"—a way of viewing the world that is different.

Let's take a closer look at David's perspectacles and how David responds to being confronted and insulted not only by his brother Eliab but also by King Saul who questions David's ability to fight

Goliath. Eliab insults David by questioning his very presence at the battlefield: "With whom have you left those few sheep in the wilderness? I know your presumption and the evil of your heart; for you have come down just to see the battle."

David's answer? "What have I done now? It was only a question." (Ah, but as we have seen, it was so much more than a question that David was asking. He was making statements, taking a stance!)

So David turns away from Eliab, toward someone else. He "spoke in the same way," asking again, "what shall be done for the man who kills this uncircumcised Philistine?"

Remember, David already knows the answer to that question. The soldiers told him when he first arrived that anyone who kills Goliath will receive an enormous reward from the king: huge wealth, no taxes, and the king's own daughter in marriage. He heard it the first time and he already asked them to repeat it, which they did. But here he is, asking the question again, making a point, sharing a perspective, that Goliath is uncircumcised and therefore unprotected. And for the third time, David doesn't focus on the things that diminish and discourage the soldiers (Goliath's size and intimidating words) but rather encourages them, reminding the soldiers of the king's generous reward.

You see what is going on here? Look at David's reaction when faced with efforts at sabotage:

✔ He does not get defensive.

✔ He does not trade insult for insult.

✔ He does not even address the accusation made against him.

✔ He simply turns away from his accuser and keeps asking the same question as before.

What a great model.

There is very little (or nothing) to be gained from engaging with those who seek to sabotage us when we offer to step up and slay a Goliath. Sure, if someone offers in a helpful, constructive way a criticism or critique of the way you are proposing to attack your giant, you should listen. But that is not what is going on here between David and his brother. Eliab is not saying, *Listen, David, we've been out here studying Goliath's armor, and the way he stands, and we think we've discovered a weakness. Before you go on running your mouth anymore, can we share with you what we have learned?*

That would be constructive criticism, or at least the start of it, and far from the insults, accusations, and bitterness that David encounters from his brother.

How do you know the difference?

When you offer an idea—when you put yourself out there and make yourself vulnerable by sharing an idea or a strategy—and someone reacts to it, pay attention to your gut. Your gut, your intuition, knows the difference between constructive criticism and jealous attempts to sabotage. If you get a reaction totally out of proportion, then chances are you have touched a nerve—someone else's nerve—and their opposition has very little to do with what you've actually proposed.

Understanding that his brother is engaging in sabotage, David does not get defensive. He refuses to engage in a verbal spar with his accuser. He turns away. Before long, King Saul hears about David wandering around and asking questions. And he sends for him.

David goes to Saul and tells him two things: One, that no one should lose heart because of Goliath, and two, that he, David, will go and fight this Philistine himself.

Saul's response is not so encouraging for David, at least not at first. King Saul's immediate reaction is to tell David that David doesn't have a chance: "You can't go and fight this Philistine. You're too young and inexperienced—and he's been at this fighting business since before you were born" (1 Samuel 17:33, *The Message*).

Once again, the boldness and courage in David's offer to fight Goliath are met with skepticism and doubt: In effect, Saul says to David: *You can't. You can't fight with him. You're just a boy. And Goliath, well, he's a seasoned soldier, he's been fighting since he was a kid.*

Again, let's pause at this point in the story and speculate about how David could have heard Saul's words and reacted to them.

First, the good news: at least what King Saul says is factual. Unlike Eliab's comments, what Saul says is not a mean-spirited accusation. David is young. David is completely inexperienced in hand-to-hand combat. Goliath is in fact a seasoned soldier, a champion, who has presumably fought and won hundreds of bloody battles.

And in Saul's defense, remember what's at stake: This is a winner-take-all battle, with Saul's entire army, kingdom, and population at stake. Is he really going to immediately say, *Sure, kid, go for it!*?

David seems to know the difference. So he listens to Saul's objections. His gut tells him that unlike Eliab, Saul has a valid point. Saul may not be encouraging, but he is speaking the truth.

When his brother Eliab sought to sabotage, David was wise to turn away, ignore him, and focus his attention elsewhere. But that is not what is going on with King Saul, so that same strategy would not be wise here. David realizes that another strategy is needed: David realizes Saul needs to be convinced, not ignored.

So David says to Saul,

> Your servant has been keeping his father's sheep. When a lion or a bear came and carried off a sheep from the flock, I went after it, struck it and rescued the sheep from its mouth. When it turned on me, I seized it by its hair, struck it and killed it. Your servant has killed both the lion and the bear; this uncircumcised Philistine will be like one of them, because he has defiled the armies of the living God. (1 Samuel 17:34-36, NIV)

And then David adds this: "The Lord who rescued me from the paw of the lion and the paw of the bear will rescue me from the hand of this Philistine" (17:35, NIV).

What is the very next word we hear from Saul? "Go."

"Go, and the Lord be with you," he says to David.

Wow, what happened there? What brought about such a huge change—from a vote of no confidence to a startling, sudden, and completely opposite decision, with a command to go?

What was it that David did that made Saul change his mind so radically? Let's take a closer look.

First, when David hears Saul's objection that he is only an inexperienced boy, David does not argue. He can't argue with facts, and he doesn't try. Rather, the first thing that David does is refer to himself as King Saul's servant.

Those are powerful and humble words, especially to a king. The kid may be young, he may be inexperienced in hand-to-hand combat, but he is a known entity, a loyal subject. He has been the king's servant, after all—someone who has been playing the lyre for him, comforting him, driving away evil spirits. King Saul might have thought subconsciously when he heard those words, *This kid does seem to have a powerful connection to the Lord God, because whenever he plays, evil spirits leave me alone, and I feel relief. I guess I should pay attention.*

Second, David draws on the experience he does have, saying essentially, *Your servant has been keeping his father's sheep. I have fought lions and bears. And won.*

You see the benefit of the perspectacles David is wearing? While everyone else views Goliath as unique —no one has ever met a challenge like him before—David views Goliath in the light of similar past experiences.

NEW PERSPECTACLES ——————————

I have J.D. to thank for giving me new perspectacles.

I often worry on Sundays before the 9 a.m. service begins in the main sanctuary. That sanctuary seats 900 people, and we started our first Sunday with forty-five. In just a couple of years, we are up to 120 regulars at that service, with forty-four children in Sunday school. But even with this growth and even though we have rearranged chairs and tried to make the space feel more intimate, it is a huge space. And God forgive me but sometimes I don't see the 100 who are there as much as I see the 800 empty chairs.

Adding to my stress: People at this service, many of them harried parents juggling lots of responsibilities, don't show up on time. At five minutes to 9 a.m., oftentimes there are only about 30 people in church. By the time the opening procession is over and I turn around, I am shocked to see the number quadrupled. But before the service begins, I am often standing there fighting back panic: "This is IT. This is all who are coming. Ever. We're going to fail."

One Sunday late in 2012, a minute or two after 9, I was standing there, looking at the small crowd, thinking they were all we would have that day. I was thinking that the honeymoon was over; it had all been a flash in the pan.

Externally, I was fine: calm, cool, collected. Smiling, even. But internally, this Sunday, I was freaking out. About to throw up. I felt like a failure—a spectacular, expensive, public failure.

That's when J.D., a longtime parishioner who happened to be ushering that day, turned to me and said, "Wow! Look at all these people! This is wonderful."

I thought she was mocking me.

But she was smiling in a way that made me look out at the congregation. I realized that only a handful of the people in the pew were "continuing congregation" folk. About thirty were new. And that was indeed wonderful.

Thanks to her perspective, I was able to calm down and see the good news right in front of me.

While everyone else views Goliath as incomparable, David takes a minute to step back and compare. He compares Goliath to lions (which can stretch to over eight feet in length) and to bears (which can stand to nearly nine feet in height), both of which he has encountered in the past—and has defeated.

Again, David is a great model, teaching us something important about the giants we face in life: Part of what makes the giants in our life seem so terrifying is the thought that we have never encountered anything like them before. Yes, the size of our giant is intimidating, but what makes it even more intimidating is the thought that we are in new territory, that all bets are off, that our past experience, wisdom, and resources are of no use to us in this battle. The unknown is a frightening place.

David, however, reminds us of the power of comparison. He doesn't allow himself to become paralyzed by the fear that comes from thinking he is out of his league. Rather, he compares the problem he is facing to ones he has faced and overcome before.

And notice this: David doesn't worry that the comparison is not an exact one. Okay, it is technically true that he has never faced a ten-foot tall human being before, much less a ten-foot, battle-hardened soldier. But he doesn't allow himself to get bogged down in that distinction. He thinks of how this new problem might be similar to old problems he has faced—and overcome.

But there is a much more important point. And that is to whom David gives credit for his ability to survive attacks by lions and bears: "The Lord who rescued me from the paw of the lion and the paw of the bear will rescue me from the hand of this Philistine," he says.

David compares his past experiences of being rescued by God to the way he believes he will be rescued by God in his fight with Goliath.

In other words, David does not allow the doubt and reservations expressed by his brother and Saul to unnerve him. Basically, he understands: It's not about him. Instead, it is about God: the God who rescued David in the past and the God who will rescue him again now and in the future.

Giants, seemingly insurmountable problems in life, are a given. What makes David different—and what can make us different—is what we measure those giants against. If we measure giants against our own size, our own abilities, our own resources, we are understandably intimidated, disheartened, and afraid to act or move.

David teaches us to shift our focus and our frame of reference. He teaches us to see that a problem might look big to us, but how big is it to God? David's boldness and our own comes from measuring giants against God's size and not our own. Self-confidence is important, but if we're going to slay a Goliath, there has to be more than self-confidence: There has to be God-confidence.

So it is David's God-confidence that convinces Saul. It is David's God-confidence that persuades Saul to tell David to "go"—go fight Goliath.

But something has to happen first: Before slaying his Goliath, David must first reject Saul's armor and then pick his five smooth stones.

FOR FURTHER REFLECTION:

1. Reflect on David's reaction when faced with Eliab's sabotage:

✔ He does not get defensive.

✔ He does not trade insult for insult.

✔ He doesn't even address the accusation made against him.

✔ He simply turns away from his accuser/attacker and keeps asking the same question as before.

When faced with sabotage, which reactions are you most likely to have? Defensiveness? Lashing back? Arguing your side? Focusing your attention on the criticizer? Have you found these responses helpful? How did others react to your response?

2. How do you distinguish between a saboteur and someone you simply need to spend time convincing?

3. Reflect on experiences when you have faced giants and overcome them. What helped you deal with those giants? Are there times you felt the giants won? What can you learn from these experiences as you address the giants you are facing now?

4. Often people don't recognize God's power except in hindsight. Looking back over your life, where and how has God helped you or those you know slay giants? Do these past experiences help you trust God for the future? Why or why not?

CHAPTER 6

REJECT SAUL'S ARMOR, THEN PICK
YOUR FIVE SMOOTH STONES

Finally King Saul agrees to let David fight Goliath. Before David goes, however, an odd scene unfolds.

In a well-intentioned gesture, Saul dresses David in his kingly armor. Saul puts a bronze helmet on David's head. He clothes David with his coat of armor. David fastens Saul's sword over the armor. Then David tries walking around. But he can't. Scripture tells us, "He tried in vain to walk, for he was not used to them."

David says to Saul, "I cannot walk with these; for I am not used to them."

David takes off Saul's armor. He rejects it.

In the story, Saul's armor is literal—an actual helmet, suit, and sword that Saul tried equipping David with before the battle. But Saul's armor is also a rich metaphor for us today, symbolizing all sorts of things:

✔ Saul's assistance that David has to reject because he needs to show Saul he doesn't need help to defeat Goliath.

✔ Military might and protection that David has to reject because he trusts in God as his protector and shield.

✔ The trappings of Saul's earthly kingship that David has to reject because he believes in the Lord God as his king.

Each of these interpretations seems valid. I wouldn't argue with any of them. Still I prefer a different take on Saul's armor. These interpretations cast Saul's armor in a negative light, as if there is something inherently wrong with it. But in the story, Saul's armor doesn't seem to have any inherent moral value at all. In other words, Saul's armor itself is neither good nor bad: It is a collection of metal and leather.

In fact, when Saul wore Saul's armor, it protected him. It probably gave him confidence. If Saul went into battle without his armor, it is likely he would be seriously injured or killed.

What is wrong with Saul's armor is that it does not fit David. David, after all, is a shepherd. He is not accustomed to wearing armor. Had Saul insisted on David wearing his armor (or had David not insisted on rejecting it), David would have lumbered out to Goliath, clunking one foot in front of the other, struggling to see, struggling even to keep his balance.

But after trying Saul's armor on and trying to walk around in it, David recognizes how ill-fitting it is. Then he rejects it.

He literally takes it off; he removes it. He takes the armor from his own body and gives it back to Saul.

This part of the story teaches us an important life lesson about how to reject armor without rejecting the person. That is, how can we decline things that have been and may still be useful to others but don't fit us without rejecting the Saul who offers these things?

What an important lesson to learn and implement. A lot of well-intentioned Sauls in our lives will encourage us to try on what has worked well for them:

- ✔ We are asked to try on certain types of religious thinking.

- ✔ We slip into old organizational or business models.

- ✔ We find ourselves clothed in longstanding customs, wearing other people's mentalities, rules, regulations, concepts, or structures.

There is a story you may have heard that makes this point in a humorous way. It is about a young newlywed couple. One night they were making dinner and the husband noticed his wife cutting off both ends of the ham, about a quarter of the ham on each end, leaving only the middle half. He was baffled, and said to her, "Why are you cutting off the ends of the ham?"

His wife looked surprised but thoughtful and said, "Hmm…I don't know. My mother always did it, though."

A few months later, he was over at his mother-in-law's home, and so he said; "Hey, I'm curious: Why do you cut the ends of the ham off before you bake it?" She had a similar look on her face but after thinking for a few minutes said, "Well, because my mother always did."

Time passed, and there was a family reunion, and grandmother was present. The young man was still curious, so he asked her the same question that had perplexed him: "When you bake a ham, why do you cut the ends of the ham off?"

Grandmother confidently answered, "Because my pan was too small."

> So many times we unthinkingly try to "wear" what has fit
> or worked well for others. The question is, does it fit for
> us? Does it make sense for us? Does it work for us? If not,
> we need to have David's wisdom and courage to reject it.

Let's look at two concrete examples of this dynamic, of times when
we may need to reject Saul's armor while not rejecting the Saul who
offers it.

The first example is one close to my heart, and that is the practice of
prayer. While there are many reasons or motivations to pray, it seems
fair to say that the purpose of prayer is to bring us into the presence
of God, to change and transform us, and then to send us out into the
world to love and serve God and our neighbors.

But so often, prayer does not do that. When we pray, we don't sense
we are in the closer presence of God. Or we don't find that prayer is
transforming our lives for the better. Why?

Well, often it is because we have come to believe that we must pray in
a certain way, or use certain words, or have a certain posture, or pray
at a certain time. And why do we believe these things? Often it is
because well-intentioned Sauls in our lives offered us their armor—
books and techniques that work well for them—and they encouraged
us to try that armor on for ourselves.

Again, this might be just fine. If someone else's way of praying fits
you, if it works well for you, if it allows you to get in touch with God,
be transformed by God, and helps you become a better, more loving
person, then accept the gift!

But if you find, like David, that you can't move around in someone else's way of praying, if it is ill-fitting and uncomfortable, then you should, like David, reject it.

In the early 1980s, an ancient style of prayer called centering prayer became very popular again. A Trappist monk by the name of Basil Pennington published a book called *Centering Prayer*, and it sold over a million copies.

During those years, many people whom I admired embraced centering prayer. They seemed to be holy, calm, centered, loving, and peaceful people. And centering prayer helped them be that way.

At that time, I was seldom calm, seldom centered, seldom loving, and rarely peaceful. I wanted what those people had. And since they seemed to get it from centering prayer, I eagerly accepted their suggestions to try it on myself. So I tried. I sat still. I found a word on which to concentrate. I read and reread the books my friends recommended.

But for me, centering prayer was not serving prayer's purpose: It was not putting me in closer touch with God. It was not making me a more loving person. For me, centering prayer was Saul's armor, something I had to set aside. I removed it from my daily routine. I politely thanked the people who suggested new ways of trying it, but I also let them know it wasn't for me.

Well, you know how they say that when the student is ready, the teacher will appear? Sure enough, not long after I turned away from centering prayer, I met a Jesuit priest who introduced me to Ignatian prayer. The core of Ignatian spirituality is "finding God in all things," rooted not so much in centering one's self, but in a short daily *examen* in which you reflect on the ways that God was present in the past twenty-four hours of your life.

This style of prayer instantly fit me. I read and reread (and still reread) a book by William Barry, SJ, titled *Finding God in All Things*, which has become a kind of bedrock of my prayer life. I have met with an Ignatian spiritual director almost every month for the past twenty years, and I have gone on several Ignatian retreats.

I am still far from being a holy person. But I find that when I stick to this style of prayer, it works for me: It has a remarkable way of allowing me to get in touch with God. It allows me to be transformed by God. It helps me become, by God's grace, a better, more loving person.

Now in saying all this—in sharing my enthusiasm for what I have found—I am not forcing Ignatian prayer on you. You might find it to be YOUR Saul's armor! What worked for others didn't work for me, and what works for me might not work for you. The point is, we each have our own armor to reject.

A second example of a time we may need to reject Saul's armor while not rejecting the person who offers it is in regard to leadership. One thing that all leaders have in common is that they need to rally their followers. However, there is an all-too-human tendency that many leaders have inherited, and that is to define their organization or cause by what they are not and to rally their followers against a common enemy. I call this enemy-based leadership.

I am talking about the mentality that causes a leader to proclaim, "We are not _____ (fill in the blank), and therefore we must rally against 'those people.'"

Whether the followers are parishioners, constituents, customers, athletes, or students, the dynamic is the same. The enemy-based leader focuses people on a common enemy.

We know the dynamic all too well: The cry goes out: "We are not _____, and therefore we must rally against the Protestants (or Catholics), the conservatives (or liberals), Mac (or PC), Red Sox (or Yankees).

This kind of enemy-based leadership is common and tempting for at least three reasons:

- ✔ It's fast. It quickly gives people a sense of identity around which they can rally: "We are who we are because we are not them."

- ✔ It's lucrative. It brings in the cash. Leaders can raise lots of money by appealing to our innate fear of the other. "If we don't raise enough financial resources to fight those people, then they are going to win."

- ✔ It's easy: It relieves a leader from having to do the difficult work of self-identifying and then improving who or what one actually is or stands for.

Enemy-based leadership may be fast, lucrative, and easy, but it is not the only version of leadership there is, and I don't think it is the best.

Another version of leadership is what I call vision-based leadership. These leaders define themselves and their organization or cause by what they are and rally their followers toward a common vision.

I am talking about a mentality that causes a leader to proclaim, "We believe in _____" or "We stand up for _____." Or when a business leader says, "Our product makes your life better by _____" or when a coach says "Our team seeks to live into [this tradition] " or when educators say "Our institution improves the world by _____."

This kind of vision-based leadership is less common, for the opposite reasons:

✔ It is slow. Developing a sense of identity around a common vision is time-consuming. It takes time to get lots of people involved in the process of identifying values they have in common.

✔ It is less lucrative, at least at first. Cash will pour in, but only after the message gets out, and trusting relationships are built. Leaders need to raise money by appealing to common values or hopes.

✔ It is difficult. A leader must do the hard work of determining, through an iterative process of reflection and study, who he or she actually is or what his or her organization actually stands for.

A leader's first step in adopting vision-based leadership is to reject the armor of enemy-based leadership.

Defining a faith community by who is "out"—who is less orthodox or less progressive—may have worked for faith communities in the past (and may still work for some now). But if you are a religious leader who has tried that method and now you find that you "cannot walk" in that strategy—it doesn't fit you, limits you, and is turning off more people than it is attracting—then you need to reject that Saul's armor.

OUR OWN DIRECTION

In August of 2013, about a year into my ministry at The Falls Church Episcopal, leaders of The Falls Church Anglican decided to continue litigating what had already been a seven-year long case of who owns Episcopal Church property.

Earlier that year, the Supreme Court of Virginia issued a unanimous ruling in favor of our diocese and The Falls Church Episcopal and against the case of the so-called "breakaway" parish. The Anglican leaders of the breakaway church notified members that they planned to appeal the case to the Supreme Court of the United States.

Talk about facing a Goliath. It was a very discouraging time, for me personally, and for our parish.

In response, I sent a message to my congregation. I offered the congregation a bit of context. I reminded them why we were in this legal battle: People are free to leave a church or a denomination if they have differences of opinion, but at least in The Episcopal Church, they are not free to claim church property as their own. In fact, even though we had returned to our church property in 2012, we were clear that the property wasn't ours either. Rather, we think of ourselves as caretakers, people entrusted to take care of property that previous generations of Episcopalians built, maintained, and left for future generations of Episcopalians.

So there we were, back in our property, but with news that the legal case was going to drag on, and no one knew for how long. Probably years. So, what to do in the meantime?

Perhaps because our daughter, Elizabeth, was getting her driver's license, I was reminded of something that you teach beginning drivers. If you're driving at night, and someone is coming the opposite direction with their bright lights or high beams on, you must resist the temptation to stare at those lights.

It is human nature to move toward that which we concentrate on. If you stare at the bright lights, you will be drawn into them, perhaps dangerously so. We must, I wrote, learn to look away from the annoyance and distraction of the lawsuit and instead concentrate on the road on which we are driving and the direction in which we are going.

Thanks to the prayerful and hard work of the vestry, we had completed a three-to-five year vision process. For the past year, we had spent time asking what God's will might be for our particular faith community at this particular time.

We came up with five visions, or directions, we believed we were called to go. We tested these visions or directions in a series of dinners and listening sessions over the course of several months. And based on congregational feedback, we added a sixth. (These visions—directions—can be found in the Appendix).

One day soon, I told my congregation, the bright, distracting lights of litigation will have passed. We cannot ignore those lights, but neither should we concentrate on, or be drawn into, them.

Instead, we decided to go pedal-to-the-metal on our own road. We had exciting places to go.

Similarly, partisanship may have worked for others in the past (and may still work for some now). But a political leader may need to reject the Saul's armor of partisanship if it is causing frustration and gridlock instead of promoting peace and prosperity.

And the same goes for CEO's, clergy, coaches, academic deans, and other leaders: If business models, religious doctrines, playbooks, or policies have been tried but are not furthering the ideals of the institution, it's time to state the truth, "I cannot walk in these." It is time to reject Saul's armor in whatever form it takes.

In doing so, however, it is important to remember how David rejected Saul's armor. He did not criticize it; he did not make fun of it; he certainly did not disparage Saul for offering it to him. David even tried on the armor, and he walked around in it. That was respectful to Saul.

But he only walked around in it for a little bit. Once he knew Saul's armor didn't fit him, he didn't prolong the process of rejecting it. And he certainly did not keep wearing the armor out of some false sense of loyalty to Saul.

What a great lesson for us. Just as Saul's armor was just metal and leather—nothing inherently right or wrong with the armor itself—there may be nothing inherently wrong with a religious, political, business, sports, or academic strategy we have inherited. We should, like David, try different strategies on, and if they fit us well, we should wear them.

But if after walking around a bit, you find yourself stifled, cramped, confined, restrained—if the strategy is not serving its purpose—then don't keep it on out of some sense of duty to the past. State the truth. Reject it. Take it off.

But take off the armor with grace. It takes a great deal of diplomacy to reject Saul's armor without rejecting Saul who, with good intentions, offered the armor. Unnecessary hurt feelings, heartaches, and fights erupt when we don't remember the difference between rejecting Saul's armor and rejecting Saul. Remember, David doesn't spend any time criticizing Saul's armor; David simply points out that it doesn't fit him, that he cannot move in it.

> And finally we arrive at the reason it is so important to reject Saul's armor: It is to be free, like David, to select our own five smooth stones.

As the story picks up again, that is exactly what David does: "Then he took his staff in his hand, and chose five smooth stones from the wadi, and put them in his shepherd's bag, in the pouch; his sling was in his hand, and he drew near to the Philistine."

What wonderful, practical guidance this gives you as you go out to face your giant! First, consider how personal this sentence is. It is no longer about Saul, Saul's equipment, or Saul's talent. It is about David, David's equipment, and David's talent. David takes his staff in hand, and he chooses, for himself, five smooth stones from the wadi. He equips himself with these stones; he puts them in the pouch of his shepherd's bag, and with his sling in his hand, he goes out to battle Goliath.

Second, look at how deliberate David is. David doesn't randomly pick up rocks from along the path leading to the riverbank. No, drawing on his expertise with a sling shot, he selects stones that the waters have turned smooth. He picks stones that he knows will fit in his slingshot. He knows which stones fly well through the air and which ones, if thrown with enough precision and force, can become powerful and even deadly weapons.

In picking your five smooth stones, remember David and his process. First, make it personal. It is no longer about whatever Saul's armor you have rejected. That is done. Now it is time for you to focus on your passion.

In his book, *Wild at Heart*, author John Eldredge writes:

> If you had permission to do what you really wanted to do, what would you do? Don't ask how—"how" cuts desire off at the knees. In the beginning of asking yourself what you want to do, asking how you're going to do it is faithlessness. "How" is God's department. He is asking you WHAT. What is written in your heart? What makes you come alive? If you could do what you've always wanted to do, what would it be? (A clue: those times you found yourself loving what you were doing.) Release control in exchange for the recovery of the dreams in your heart.

To find your five smooth stones, ask: What gets you out of bed in the morning? What animates you, motivates you, excites you? What comes naturally to you?

Second, like David, be deliberate. David had no expertise in hand-to-hand human combat, but he did have expertise in fighting bears and lions. And that is the experience David focused upon. After you have spent time discerning your passions, focus on what you are equipped with and talented at. This will be different from others. Carefully consider your own gifts and talents.

Don't forget the ordinary—the things you do on a daily basis, maybe even without giving them much thought. Recall that David attacked Goliath with what he already had in his hand: his staff and his sling. His everyday tools.

Allow yourself, likewise, to answer the question: What is in my hand? What are those things I am already carrying, already good at? How do I spend the majority of my waking hours? What expertise or wisdom have I gained from that?"

The answers to those questions will help you find more of your five smooth stones—stones that God will use to help you face your giant. That is, as long as you are putting your trust in the right place.

SMOOTH STONES

One of the Goliaths that we faced—and still face—at Falls Church Episcopal and across The Episcopal Church is an impression, unfortunately sown by those who disagree with us, that we are a church that does not take the Bible seriously. That we don't respect scriptural authority. That because of the way we interpret scripture, we are unorthodox, engaged in false teaching, or even heretical.

While there are certainly some unorthodox members and even leaders in The Episcopal Church, I think this is a misleading narrative about us. So some time ago, I decided that instead of getting frustrated with those accusations, I would address that Goliath-of-a-narrative head on.

I have come to believe the accusations present a good opportunity to focus on three things:

- ✔ What Episcopalians believe about the Bible
- ✔ How we should read the Bible
- ✔ What we believe about the authority and role of scripture

WHAT EPISCOPALIANS BELIEVE ABOUT THE BIBLE

We believe the book called the Bible is the Word of God.

The Bible, of course, is not one book, but more than sixty books of history, prophecy, poetry, prose, narrative, and correspondence. In his book, *Wishful Thinking*, American theologian Frederick Buechner writes:

> There are people who say we should read the Bible as literature. ...Read the Bible for the story it tells. Read the King James Version especially for the power of its prose and the splendor of its poetry. Read it for the history it contains and for its insights into ancient ways. Don't worry about whatever it is supposed to mean to religious faith. Don't bother about the hocus-pocus. Read it like any other book.
>
> The trouble is it's not like any other book. To read the Bible as literature is like reading *Moby Dick* as a whaling manual or *The Brothers Karamazov* for its punctuation.
>
> It is a book about the sublime and the unspeakable, about life the way it really is. It is a book about people who at one and the same time can be both believing and unbelieving, innocent and guilty, crusaders and crooks, full of hope and full of despair.
>
> In other words, it's a book about us.

HOW WE SHOULD READ THE BIBLE

First of all, we should read it! I wish people would spend less time defending the authority of scripture and more time actually reading it.

But not just any way of reading it will do. If you try to plow your way through, you will get bogged down after Exodus and never want to pick it up again.

I encourage people to find a good, readable Bible. Don't try to read it all in one sitting; it is far better to savor one chapter or even one verse and really let the words seep in than to force your eyes through every page. If you need help in this, find someone to help you.

And don't be afraid to wrestle with scripture. It is the Word of God, and God can handle it. Ask questions, probe, challenge. Ask "so what?" Make scripture applicable to you and your life where you really are.

WHAT WE BELIEVE ABOUT THE AUTHORITY AND ROLE OF SCRIPTURE

This is the trickiest question. Let me start by saying our faith is not in the Bible but in God who inspired the Bible and to whom the Bible points.

Let me repeat that: Our faith is not in the Bible but in God who inspired the Bible and to whom the Bible points.

Imagine a group of people gathered under a huge sign that says, "Dining Hall: 200 yards," with an arrow pointing to the right. You walk up to this group of people and ask, "What are you doing here?"

They say, "We're hungry, and we want to eat."

You say, "Well, the Dining Hall is that way." They respond, "No, it says 'Dining Hall' right there—this must be it!"

Imagine your frustration in trying to get them to focus not on the sign, but on what they're searching for—what the sign is pointing to.

Buechner expresses this same frustration: "If you look at a window, you see flyspecks, dust, the crack where Junior's Frisbee hit it. If you look through the window, you see the world beyond."

The Bible is a sign pointing to the Living God. In other words, scripture is the truth, and that truth is unchanging, but this unchanging truth must in every age be received, interpreted, and applied.

There are some very clear and explicit passages in the Bible that contain teachings about the proper role, or lack thereof, of women in the church, the inappropriateness of remarriage after divorce, and the Bible's acceptance of the institution of slavery. (And I haven't even touched scriptural passages on wealth, which probably outweigh passages on sex by a hundred to one.)

The point I'm making is twofold:

First, the use, or misuse, of scripture by proof-texting is the dynamic that happens whenever people gather around a sign and point at the sign instead of the place or person to whom the sign points.

Second, over the years, the Church has found ways to uphold the truth of the Bible while saying that this truth must in every age be received and interpreted. You may not agree with The Episcopal Church's decisions to bless same-sex unions and advocate for gay marriage, but my point is that when we uphold the truth of the Bible while receiving and interpreting it in our age, we are no different than previous generations.

If the Bible is not the Word of God, if it is just another great book, then I am in the wrong vocation. But if the Bible is not seen as something alive, flexible, complex, and generous, then how will it be relevant in our everyday lives?

There is a line about The Episcopal Church I never grow tired of repeating. The sign out front says, "The Episcopal Church Welcomes You." There is no asterisk after the "you."

No matter who you are or where you are in your spiritual journey, you are welcome here. We mean that, no matter who you are. Conservative or liberal; gay or straight; Democrat, Republican, independent, Tea Party; black, white, Hispanic, Asian; married, single, divorced, separated, widowed; ninety-four years old or a newborn infant; energetic or exhausted; deeply involved in ministry or anonymously slipping in and out of worship; hearing or hearing impaired; fundamentalist or agnostic; adulterer-liar-cheater or faithful-truthful-honest; saint or sinner; confused or confident, YOU. ARE. WELCOME. HERE. No matter who you are, or where you are, God will meet you here. But (thanks be to God) through Holy Scripture, through the church's sacraments, and through God's Church, God will not leave you here. No matter who you are, or where you are in your spiritual journey, God will transform you, and me, and us, into the better souls God wants us to be.

Those are our smooth stones—at The Falls Church Episcopal and across The Episcopal Church. We arm ourselves with this as we run toward the Goliath of a false narrative.

FOR FURTHER REFLECTION:

1. What are some examples of Saul's armor—spiritual practices, worship styles, or prayer disciplines—that you have tried in the past but you found didn't fit? Which ones did?

2. Are there other types of armor—activities that might strengthen your relationship with God and enable you to battle your giants—that you would like to try on for size?

3. David found his five smooth stones—tools that fit him and would arm him against Goliath—after traveling into the valley. This was a risky endeavor, with David exposing himself to potential attack when he stepped out of the safety of the encampment. In what ways do we make ourselves vulnerable when we step out of our comfort zones to find the answers we seek?

4. David rejected Saul's armor in favor of five smooth stones. Does the fact that he opted for arms over armor—something active versus something passive, something proactive versus something reactive —resonate with you? Why or why not? How are we called to be active participants in our own salvation?

CHAPTER 7

WHAT GOD DO YOU PUT YOUR TRUST IN?

So far in the story, we have seen:

- ✔ David is not intimidated by Goliath's size, not because he thinks he measures up, but because he is comparing Goliath to God.

- ✔ David is confident that he can take Goliath on, not because he thinks he is a better fighter, but because he knows that he has divine protection and Goliath does not.

- ✔ David is confident in his slingshot, not because he is a talented marksman, but because he is confident that God used it to protect him from bears and lions.

Over and over, we see that what makes David stand out from all the others in the story is David's trust in God. And so David and Goliath finally face each other.

> His sling was in his hand, and he drew near the Philistine. The Philistine came on and drew near to David, with his shield-bearer in front of him. When the Philistine looked and saw David, he disdained him, for he was only a youth, ruddy and handsome in appearance. The Philistine said to David, "Am I a dog, that you come to me with sticks?"

David moves up from the riverbed toward Goliath, alone. Goliath and his shield-bearer move down toward him. At this point in the story, they are approaching each other, presumably at the same pace. They get closer and closer to each other—perhaps they were a football field's length apart at first—until Goliath is able to see just who is coming out of the valley to challenge him. Goliath looks David over.

The Message puts it, "As the Philistine paced back and forth, his shield bearer in front of him, he noticed David. He took one look down on him and sneered—a mere youngster, apple-cheeked and peach-fuzzed."

In other words, Goliath can't believe his eyes: a young kid, coming out against him, the hero and champion, the fiercest and largest soldier? And with no armor—only a shepherd's staff? "What am I, a dog?" Goliath spits out, insulted that someone could think he could fight him so unequipped.

At one level, this part of the story is a classic study of overconfidence. Goliath cannot imagine that David, with no armor, no sword, no helmet, and all alone, has any chance at all.

Again, David is wearing perspectacles—a different way of viewing the world. These perspectacles allow David to see Goliath as vulnerable. Goliath, too, has perspectacles but his act as blinders, keeping him from seeing his own vulnerability. Goliath, going into battle, has no conscious idea that he is vulnerable; he only knows his height and his might. He's undefeated but believes he's undefeatable. And as is so often the case, Goliath's shadow side—his blindness, his weakness—is the flip side of his strength.

> At a deeper level, this story is not so much about physical force or military might, or even psychological blind spots. It is a spiritual story. It is a story about spiritual power and divine protection.

That is why the story shifts quickly to focus on what some versions of the Bible call "principalities and powers" in the divine realm.

In an often-overlooked part of the story, Goliath and David take part in a pre-battle exchange of formal, detailed (and quite gory!) curses, with Goliath first invoking the power of his gods, and David invoking the power of the Lord God: "And the Philistine cursed David by his gods. The Philistine said to David, 'Come to me, and I will give your flesh to the birds of the air and to the wild animals of the field.'"

David sees Goliath's threat and raises him:

> You come to me with sword and spear and javelin; but I come to you in the name of the LORD of hosts, the God of the armies of Israel, whom you have defied. This very day the LORD will deliver you into my hand, and I will strike you down and cut off your head; and I will give the dead bodies of the Philistine army this very day to the birds of the air and to the wild animals of the earth, so that all the earth may know that there is a God in Israel, and that all this assembly may know that the LORD does not save by sword and spear; for the battle is the LORD's and he will give you into our hand.

Notice that as the exchange starts, Goliath curses David "by his gods"—plural and lower case.

While Goliath's gods are not specifically named in this story, we know from earlier in 1 Samuel (5:1-2) that there were Philistine temples to Dagon (a fish-fertility god) in the city of Ashdod, and at the very end of the book (31:8-10), we learn that Saul's dead body (and possibly head) was impaled in a temple to Astarte/Ashtaroth (a fertility, sexuality, and war goddess) in the then-Philistine-controlled fortress of Beth-Shan.

Those are the gods Goliath believes in. Those are the gods whose power Goliath invokes as he goes into battle. David, in turn, invokes the name and the power of the God he believes in.

It begs a question, a very important question: What God or gods do you trust in?

If you are familiar with the Ten Commandments, you know that the first commandment prohibits the worship of other gods. What most people may not realize, however, is that it doesn't say that there are no other gods. David, like all early Israelites, believes there are dozens, if not hundreds of gods.

I believe that there is really no such thing as an atheist. What I mean by that is I believe we all have something driving us—something or someone at the center of our hearts, some core central belief system. We may not call that something or someone a god, but that is only a matter of what vocabulary we use. The question, then, is not so much, "Do I believe in God?" but "What, or who, is the god (or who are the gods) I put my trust in?" "What is my center? What is my *raison d'être*—the most important reason or purpose for my existence?"

We human beings can run away from those questions, but we are hardwired with a mysterious hunger inside each of us, a seemingly unquenchable thirst, a deep desire, a yearning that only the Lord God can fill.

As Saint Augustine said, "You have made us for yourself, O Lord, and our hearts are restless until they rest in you."

In other words, there is a God-shaped hole in each of us that only God can fill. But we spend so much time trying to fill that hole with all kinds of things, people, and pursuits.

We are constantly searching for the latest thing that will fulfill us— fill us full or make us happy—career fulfillment, a luxury car, the newest exercise class, therapy, a new church, a new relationship, living through our kids' accomplishments, the latest cause, a home restoration, triathlons, you name it. The list is endless.

All these things are good, or at least they can be, but the question is, "Are we putting our trust in small-g 'gods'? Have they become Dagons and Ashtartes to us?"

In twenty years of parish ministry, I have come to the conclusion that there are three false, small-g gods that keep us from true joy, true happiness, and lasting fulfillment that God provides. And those three small-g gods are work, wealth, and religion.

Work, wealth, and religion: three good things that make terrible gods.

I would like to take a look at each of these false gods, and then offer an antidote, or way to counter the false god and put God back at the center of our lives.

Let us take work first.

Work is important, because for most people, it is how we spend the majority of our waking hours for forty or fifty years. And that can be a good thing. Work is, or can be, meaningful in the literal sense of that word: full of meaning. While many people work in what they consider meaningless jobs, many find work that is more than just a means to an end, something to pay the bills.

Through work, we support ourselves and our families; we can make significant contributions to our community, the nation, and even the world. And so, at least in the Judeo-Christian tradition, work is a good and even a God-given thing. God, we are told, worked in the beginning of creation, and God blesses human labor.

But like many good things, work can become our center, our primary or driving force in life. It can become the thing around which the rest of our lives revolve. Work can become something, in other words, that we bow down to: a small-g god instead of the Lord God. And while work is a good thing, it is a terrible god.

Perhaps you have heard the story about the American businessman who was at the pier of a small coastal Mexican village. A small boat with just one fisherman docked there. Inside the small boat were several, large, yellowfin tuna. The American complimented the fisherman on the quality of his fish and asked how long it took to catch them. The man said only a little while.

The American then asked, "Why didn't you stay out longer and catch more fish?"

The Mexican said he had enough to support his family's immediate needs. "I keep one fish for my family's dinner; I trade the other ones for bread and vegetables and whatever else we need for the day." The American then asked, "But what do you do with the rest of your time?"

The fisherman said, "I sleep late, fish a little, play with my children, take siesta with my wife, stroll into the village each evening where I sip wine and play guitar with my amigos. I have a full and busy life, señor."

The American scoffed, and said, "I am a Harvard MBA, and I could help you. You should spend more time fishing and instead of just bartering, sell the fish, and with the proceeds buy a bigger boat."

The fisherman was intrigued. "What then?"

"With the proceeds from the bigger boat you could buy several boats," the American said. "Eventually you would have a fleet of fishing boats. Instead of selling your catch to a middleman you would sell directly to the processor, eventually opening your own cannery. You would control the product, processing and distribution."

"Yes? What then?"

"Well, you would need to leave this village and move to Mexico City, then Los Angeles, and eventually New York City, where you would run an expanding enterprise."

The fisherman asked, "But how long will this take?"

The American said, "Oh, I'd say fifteen to twenty years."

"But what then, señor?"

The American smiled and said, "That's the best part! When the time is right, you would announce an IPO and sell your company stock to the public and become very rich, you would make millions."

"Millions?" the fisherman replied. "And then what?"

The American said, "Well, you could retire and move to a small coastal fishing village where you could sleep late, fish a little, take siesta with your wife, stroll into the village each evening to sip wine and play guitar with your friends..."

We expend a lot of effort searching for that which is right in front of us, working for that which is already ours, trying to earn that which is gift.

We, especially those of us North Americans in the twenty-first century, have a lot of trouble slowing down. We are in a hurry to do just about everything. Years ago, I heard someone on the radio being interviewed, an author who has written a book on the art of slowing down. At one point in the interview he said that we ought to find a way, as a culture, to slow down, all of us, and that as part of that effort, perhaps we could set aside, say, one day a week, to do nothing. We could call it a day of rest, in which people would do no work. Yeah, I mumbled, why didn't God think of that?

> The antidote to work as the center of our lives, a way to dethrone work as king of our hearts and put God back, is through the commandment to rest, really rest, trusting in God's care one day out of seven.

The commandment to take one day as a sabbath is designed to put us in touch, on a regular basis, with the God-shaped hole in our lives, to force us to quit doing and just be, so we are forced to ask the big questions. These include:

- ✔ What difference am I making, what difference do I make?

- ✔ Whom, or what, do I put my trust in? Who, or what, is at the center of my life? What is driving me?

- ✔ Am I living the way God wants me to live?

When we have time to ask these questions, we give space for God to speak to us, to guide us.

Another terrible god is wealth. Money is a good thing, or can be. Wealth, and the things wealth can get us, can enrich our lives and the lives of others. But money, and the things money can buy, are probably the most likely good and God-given thing that we try to stuff into our God-shaped hole.

This reminds me of another story; this one takes place at a major university. There was a huge faculty meeting, with everyone gathered around a big table. All of a sudden, in the middle of the meeting, an angel appeared out of nowhere and hovered right above the dean of faculty.

The angel says, "I have been sent to reward you for your years of dedication and hard work. I have been authorized to grant you one of three desires. You may have beauty, and be the handsomest man in the world. Or you may have money, and be the wealthiest man in the world. Or you may have wisdom, and be the wisest man in the world. Choose."

Without hesitating, the dean says, "Wisdom!"

"Granted!" the angel says, and with a poof, disappears.

The dean of faculty just sits there, with this glow all around him. The rest of the faculty just sits there, stunned, in silence. Finally, one of the faculty members says, "Say something!"

The dean says, "I should have taken the money...."

We think there is happiness in making a lot of money. Despite all evidence and other people's experience to the contrary, we think that money, or the adventures and possessions money can buy, will fill that gnawing, empty space inside of us and make us happy.

That is not to say that being poor is a recipe for happiness either. Involuntary poverty is awful. I have done work in inner-city Nashville, Tennessee, and served on the board of directors of Samaritan Ministry for the Homeless of Washington, DC. For many years, I have taken teenagers on trips to help relieve some of the extreme poverty in the Appalachian mountains, in post-Katrina New Orleans, and in far western Honduras. Those experiences have taught me not to romanticize poverty.

Part of the reason we were able to help the poor was that people with wealth helped support our efforts. As anyone who has received a grant or scholarship can tell you, wealth can accomplish a lot of good. Wealth can be a good thing, a God-given thing, even! It can bring us—and others—joy.

The danger comes when we think wealth will give us contentment, will satisfy our cravings, will fill our God-shaped hole. Like other false gods, the small-g god of wealth tends to be addictive. And the nature of addictions is that they demand more and more from us, while giving back less and less. Recovering alcoholics have a slogan: "First you have the drink; then the drink has you." If we are honest about it, this is the same with money: First we have the money, the car, the house; then the money, the car, and the house have us.

The antidote to making wealth the center of our life, the way to dethrone wealth from the throne of our heart and put God back there, is by giving away a percentage of the money—to let go of some of it. We can talk about the other ways we practice our faith all day long, we can devote a lot of time and attention to the discipline of prayer, and we can engage in acts of service to others. But if we really want to acknowledge our dependence on God, then we should let go of some of our money.

The single most liberating thing my wife and I have done in regard to money is when we made the decision (when we could least afford it) to give away 10 percent of everything that comes into our pockets.

If your cynicism level is rising, and you think I am passing the offertory plate or trying to raise money for some particular cause, let me make it clear: I don't really care who you give the money to. Pick a charity, any charity. Pick a cause, any cause, as long as it benefits others. Just get in the habit of giving away 10 percent of your income, for the sole purpose of breaking wealth's chokehold on you and as a way of acknowledging your dependence on God alone.

While we are focusing on acknowledging our dependence on God alone, let us consider the third good and God-given thing that makes a bad god. And that is religion. Perhaps like many of you reading this book, I have a love-hate relationship with religion. On the one hand, religion is my livelihood, my interest, my passion. While I did not major in religion while in college, two religion professors, Eric Dean and William C. Placher, took me under their wings and patiently mentored me. They needed patience with me, because as a freshman and sophomore in college, I frequently railed against religion, religious people, and religious hypocrisy.

One day, Professor Dean gave me a challenge that I will never forget: He said, "John, name anything that frustrates you about religion, and you can find that same frustration somewhere in scripture itself."

"Name anything," he said, "that angers you about religious people or religious hypocrisy, and you can find that same anger expressed somewhere in the Bible itself, and I might add, it will be said a good bit more eloquently."

Professor Dean knew what he was saying. His challenge led me to pick up the Bible and read it for myself. And so I read. I was particularly drawn to the prophets Amos, Hosea, and Isaiah. And there I encountered a God who, throughout history, sees things being done by religious folks that are antithetical to God's intentions.

And it is not just the prophets who attack religious hypocrisy. It is Jesus himself. I have no way of knowing your particular beliefs about Jesus. But no matter what your belief system—fellow Episcopalian, lifelong Baptist, recent convert to Catholicism, Hindu, Jew, Muslim, Unitarian, agnostic, curious atheist—I challenge you to read any of the gospels (Matthew, Mark, Luke, or John) straight through, in one sitting, and ask yourself: What image of Jesus emerges from that reading?

Most people read only short passages of the gospels divided up into distinct stories, parables, or teachings. And so we get snapshots of Jesus and of his life and ministry.

But when we read the entire gospel in one sitting, we get the motion picture of Jesus and his ministry.

When we read one gospel story, we get a good idea of one leaf, on one branch, of one tree. But when we read an entire gospel in one sitting, we see the forest.

Here is the most astonishing thing: If we read a gospel in one sitting, the picture of Jesus that emerges is not as someone who was primarily a healer, teacher, or miracle worker, but as someone who was primarily a provocateur, a radical challenger of religious status quo.

Brought up to think that Jesus was a meek, mild, soft-spoken, gatherer-of-children-into-his-lap-type person, this image surprised me. It shocked me, even. But every time I reread a gospel, any gospel (again, front-to-back and all at once), this impression of Jesus-as-provocateur jumps out at me. It is inescapable.

Time after time, Jesus deliberately provokes the scribes and Pharisees, and when he has a chance to back down, instead of retreating, he deliberately increases the stakes. Read in one sitting, the hallmark of the gospels is not (as we suppose from hearing the stories in bits and pieces) about healing the sick, feeding the crowds, or teaching the disciples. It is rather the proclamation that the kingdom of God is at hand, a topsy-turvy, radical reorienting of the world and the world's priorities.

And the hallmark of the kingdom of God? The central priority of God? Love.

One day, one of the teachers of the law came and asked Jesus, Of all the commandments, which is the most important? Of all the commandments, of all the rules in the Bible, which one is supreme, which one is the most important, which one trumps all the others?

Jesus' answer?

> The first is, 'Hear, O Israel: the Lord our God, the Lord is one; you shall love the Lord your God with all your heart, and with all your soul, and with all your mind, and with all your strength. The second is this: you shall love your neighbor as yourself. There is no other commandment greater than these' (Mark 12:29-31).

Love God; love your neighbor as yourself. All the rest is commentary.

Religion is a good thing, a God-given thing, but throughout the centuries, religion has domesticated and tamed this radical yet very simple message. Worse than that, religion itself has for many people throughout the ages taken God's rightful place at the center of our hearts, so our religion and not God becomes our reason for being, our passion.

A friend of mine once described this dynamic well. He said that at first, whenever he would sit down to pray, he would light a candle. The candle would help him focus on the fact that this was a special time to be with God, and so the candle helped him worship God. Then he found that he was paying a lot of attention to what kind of candle he should use: scented or unscented, tall or short. And so, he said, over time he found he was worshiping the candle and God. Then pretty soon, he found he was being more and more deliberate about the candle-lighting process itself, preferring to light the candle with a match instead of a butane lighter, then preferring to use a wooden match instead of a paper match. At that point, he said, he realized he was just worshiping the candle!

We are living at an extraordinary time in world history, when there is a convergence of two massive trends: a reawakening of great spiritual hunger, and at the same time, a growing indifference to denominational or even religious affiliations.

We have a generation, in other words, that is spiritually hungry, yet impatient with religion that has been worshiping the candle instead of God. This generation is in good company. Because the antidote to religion-as-a-false-god is God, God's own self, working through the broad scope of salvation history, to burn away, like a restorative forest fire, the deadwood and old growth that suffocates life on the ground.

The challenge we face is the same challenge David and Goliath faced: What god should we trust in?

To illustrate this point, several times I have preached what I call my Box and the Brick sermon. Before the sermon, I put two items up front, where everyone can see them: a cardboard box and a cinderblock brick.

I ask for a volunteer from the congregation to come forward and stand on the cardboard box. But before stepping on the box, I ask the volunteer to have a lot of faith that the box will support his or her weight without collapsing. I like to ham this up a bit: "Have faith! Really, really believe, in your heart and mind, that this box is, really is, going to support you without crushing! Have lots of faith!"

Then I ask them to stand on the box. It crushes, every time.

I then ask the volunteer to walk over to where I have placed the cinderblock brick and stand on it. But before doing so, I ask the volunteer to have just a tiny bit of faith that the brick will support his or her weight without crushing. I ask them to barely believe it. Perhaps even to doubt that it will support him or her without crushing.

Then they stand on the brick. It supports them, every time. The point? Our faith is only as strong as the object in which it is placed.

People talk about the importance of having lots of faith. But the amount of faith you have isn't nearly as important as what you are placing your faith in. You can have all kinds of faith—tons and tons of faith—in your daily horoscope, in the stock market, in your job, or other securities, in a sports role model or politician or pastor or other hero du jour. But they are all cardboard: some stronger than others, but still, all bound to collapse under life's weight.

Conversely, you can have just the tiniest bit of faith (and perhaps, because of grace, not even any faith at all!) in the Lord God. And the

Lord God is "a crag, a stronghold," a sure foundation (Psalm 31:3). As David will say later, "The LORD is my rock, my fortress, and my deliverer, my God, my rock, in whom I take refuge, my shield and the horn of my salvation, my stronghold and my refuge, my savior" (2 Samuel 22:2-3).

When facing seemingly impossible odds in life, when going out to slay our giant, whose power do we want to invoke? The God in whom David trusted or the small-g gods in whom Goliath and others trusted?

The answer will help you, like David, slay your Goliath not with self-confidence, but with God-confidence.

FOR FURTHER REFLECTION:

1. Do you find your work meaningful? In what ways?

2. Do you regularly observe sabbath? How? If you don't, how might you begin?

3. What do you think about the concept of a "God-shaped hole"? Have you experienced a God-shaped hole in your own life? How do you fill it?

4. Have you ever thought of Jesus as a provocateur? What are some examples? Do you agree with that image of Jesus? Why or why not?

5. Why do you think this generation yearns for spirituality yet rejects religion? What do you think that means for the future of faith communities?

CHAPTER 8

SLAY YOUR GOLIATH NOT WITH SELF-CONFIDENCE, BUT WITH GOD-CONFIDENCE.

We come to the climactic battle and the end of the story. David and Goliath face each other.

"When the Philistine drew nearer to meet David, David ran quickly toward the battle line to meet the Philistine."

It is another delicious bit of storytelling, so let's pay attention to the details and savor it: First, we are told that while Goliath drew nearer to attack David, David ran quickly toward the battle line.

Goliath, with his shield-bearer in front of him, advances carefully in order to attack David. He is expecting a hand-to-hand fight of some sort but is probably wondering what kind of battle this will be. David is unarmed and only a boy.

So Goliath is moving slowly and carefully but also full of self-confidence. He does, after all, have every advantage in this fight: higher ground, larger size, more experience, superior strength, better weapons.

He has every advantage except one: While Goliath is filled with self-confidence, David is filled with God-confidence. Remember, David has already been anointed by Samuel as the next king. That was a promise. More than a promise, it was a prophetic pronouncement, a message from God that one day he would rule over Israel. So while we are used to thinking of David as the huge underdog in this story, he actually has a huge advantage!

David has a strong sense of his destiny, his calling, his fate, his future. He is heading into a man-to-man fight to the death. So as the author Graham Cooke points out in *The Way of the Warrior*, David is likely thinking, *One of us is going to die. I'm destined to be king. But I'm not king yet. So Goliath, it sucks to be you right now!*

That is God-confidence. And God-confidence is what helps you run quickly toward your battle line.

I invite you to use your imagination and enter into the final scene, making it your own. To do that, freeze-frame this part of the story in your mind. Imagine Goliath, heavily armored, stomp-stomp-stomping down the hill, and David, unarmed except for his slingshot, full-out-sprinting up the hill.

Got it? Now use your imagination to make Goliath your giant—some seemingly insurmountable problem you are facing. Now imagine that the giant facing you has emblazoned, across his chest, an image or a one or two-word summary of your problem. (If it is debt you are facing, imagine dollar signs. If it is health issues, imagine a stethoscope. If it is fatigue, imagine a pair of sleepy eyes.)

Got it? Now imagine your problem, your giant, moving closer to you. Your problem, too, has every advantage in this fight: It is above you, it is bigger than you are, it is stronger than you are.

It has every advantage except one: You have God-confidence. You are measuring your giant not against your size, but God's size.

When we compare our giants to God's size, when we reject Saul's armor and pick our five smooth stones, when we put our faith in the brick foundation of the Lord God, then we, like David, have God-confidence. We have God-authority and a sense of God-destiny.

David's running toward Goliath reminds me of what they say about fighter pilots. Apparently when fighter pilots find themselves in impossible situations, outnumbered ten to one, surrounded by enemy aircraft, what do they do? They radio back: "I'm in a target-rich environment."

A target-rich environment! You are in the toughest circumstances imaginable, and what is your attitude? Wow, look at my opportunities! Which one to pick first? That is God-confidence.

So now imagine yourself, like David, sprinting up the hill toward your problem-emblazoned giant. Here is Goliath, looking at a kid not just emerging from the battle lines but running toward him. He can't believe it: For forty days, morning and night, not only has no one come out of those battle lines before, but he has also seen people run the other way! And now, here, an unarmed kid?

"David put his hand in his bag, took out a stone, slung it, and struck the Philistine on his forehead; the stone sank into his forehead, and he fell face down on the ground."

Back to your imagination. Imagine this scene taking place in slow motion: David, running, reaches into his shepherd's bag and pulls out a stone. He slides it into the leather sling and, still running, starts twirling the sling over his head. Releasing the sling at just the right second, the stone whistles through the air, a guided missile aimed directly at the one soft spot, the one opening it was meant for: Goliath's forehead. One stone, carefully chosen and skillfully slung, with divine trajectory, does the job. It sinks into Goliath's skull, either killing him immediately or, in what I think is a more accurate reading, knocking him unconscious. David then runs and stands over him. He takes hold of Goliath's sword, draws it from its sheath, and cuts off Goliath's head.

It is a gory bit of bellicose storytelling. But if we read this part of the story not just literally, but metaphorically, it makes an important point: David's stone only knocks Goliath unconscious, but it is Goliath's own sword that actually kills him.

We render our giants unconscious with God's help and the weapons we carry, but we eliminate them for good with the weapons they carry themselves.

There is a scene in the movie *Enemy of the State* that makes this point. Edward "Brill" Lyle, played by Gene Hackman, plays an ex-CIA official now trying to take on, almost single-handedly, the NSA, the CIA, and by powerful politician. He is educating Robert Clayton Dean, played by Will Smith, about modern warfare tactics:

"In guerilla warfare, you try to use your weaknesses as strengths."

"Such as?"

"Well, if they're big and you're small, then you're mobile and they're slow. You're hidden and they're exposed....You capture their weapons and you use them against them the next time. That way they're supplying you. You grow stronger as they grow weaker."

David is mobile, Goliath is slow; David is hidden, Goliath is exposed. David seizes Goliath's weapon and uses it against him. You see? If this interpretation is correct, Goliath himself supplies the weapon that David ends up using to slay him.

רוד נוכה את נולית.   I Sam. XVII: 49.   DAVID PERCUTIT GOLIATHUM.
David killeth Goliath.   *David frappe Goliath.*
David schlägt Goliath.   David slaet Goliath.

Archbishop Desmond Tutu, who won the Nobel Peace Prize for his opposition to South Africa's apartheid, said, "If these white people had intended keeping us under, they shouldn't have given us the Bible…Apartheid sought to mislead people into believing that what gave value to human beings was a biological irrelevance, really, skin color or ethnicity. And you saw how the scriptures say it is because we are created in the image of God, that each one of us is a God-carrier."

It is a recurring theme in the Bible. God uses our enemies for God's purposes:

- ✔ At the end of Genesis, Joseph, the second-most powerful person in Egypt, tells his brothers, who had earlier sold him into slavery, "Even though you intended to do harm to me, God intended it for good" (50:20).

- ✔ Pharaoh, in his attempt to eradicate the Hebrew threat by killing all their male babies, ends up bringing Moses into his own home, who would later return to tell Pharaoh, "Let my people go" (Exodus 9:1).

- ✔ The Israelites, after being enslaved for several hundred years in Egypt, plunder the Egyptians of their jewelry, silver, gold, and clothing—back pay, if you will, for centuries of free labor.

- ✔ The Roman Empire used crosses and public crucifixions as ways to intimidate the population and suppress any signs of resistance or hope; Jesus dies on one, and the cross becomes a symbol of hope.

But these are all extraordinary examples involving major biblical characters. It is fair to ask: What does God-confidence look like in our lives? How does this dynamic of our enemies supplying the very weapon we need to defeat them work in everyday life?

Let's take a seemingly insignificant example: pet peeves.

I will bet that if we are honest, almost all of us have at least one pet peeve, something that gets on our nerves. I know I have several, and I would like to tell you about a little mental trick I have been using to overcome them, a trick I call my "Judo" reaction.

I don't know a lot about Judo, but I do know that in this particular martial art, great attention is paid to the fact that every strength has a weakness and that every forceful move creates an imbalance that can be capitalized upon by yielding to it until the imbalance is turned to one's advantage. In other words, Judo uses opponents' size and brute force against them, so they are supplying the very thing we need to defeat them.

How does this work with pet peeves? Well, whenever you find yourself irritated by something, pause for a second and notice that you are being bothered. Then ask yourself, "What is it that bothers me about that?"

If we take a moment to contemplate the question, we realize the action itself is not so bothersome as what the action represents. That is because most pet peeves are not really about the thing itself but about some underlying vice that bothers us. So when we encounter a pet peeve, we can take a moment to ask ourselves, "What is it, really, that bothers me? What is the underlying vice?"

Once we have determined that, we can ask, "Okay, what is the opposite virtue of that vice, and how can I practice it in my life?"

Do you see the Judo in this? Let's say your pet peeve is the recent trend of people saying "Happy Holidays" instead of "Merry Christmas" or "Happy Hanukkah." If that is your pet peeve, you have a choice: You can grouse about it, or you can use Judo against it. If you decide to use Judo against it, the first step is, when you find yourself irritated, to pause and think, "Okay, what is it that bothers me about that greeting?"

You give it some thought. You decide what bothers you is the superficiality of the greeting. So then you think, "Well, the root of the word holidays is holy-days. And so people are actually saying 'Happy holy days.' Hey! That overworked clerk just said, 'Happy holy days' to me!"

And then, to complete the Judo move, you think, "If 'Happy Holidays' is superficial, then what is the opposite virtue of the vice of superficiality? The answer: holiness. Well, how can I practice holiness in my life? Maybe by realizing that each of us is a God-carrier and to look for the holy in others."

Or take one of my own small pet peeves: People who, after shopping at the grocery store, abandon their shopping cart in the parking lot. I can have a choice: I can get irritated about it, or I can pause and ask myself, "What is it that bothers me about that?"

Let's say that what bothers me about abandoned shopping carts is the underlying vice of inconsideration. So, what is the opposite virtue? Helpfulness. I can practice helpfulness by gathering those abandoned carts on my way to the corral, helping some overworked grocery store clerk in the meantime, and for bonus points, I can pick up some litter along the way, making life just a bit easier for someone.

In the scripture passage, we see a sudden morale shift in both armies after David slays Goliath.

"When the Philistines saw that their champion was dead, they fled. The troops of Israel and Judah rose up with a shout and pursued the Philistines as far as Gath and the gates of Ekron."

David's actions, rooted in God-confidence, have a ripple effect: They not only bring about the death of Goliath but also cause a previously emboldened Philistine army to suddenly turn and run—and a previously demoralized Israelite army to surge forward.

> Our final lesson here is this: You can bet that whenever you step up to slay your Goliath, people are watching. Your actions do not take place in a vacuum; they are being watched by people who need encouragement.

You are meant, in other words, to be a source of light to others. In Isaiah, God tells the Israelites: "I will give you as a light to the nations, that my salvation may reach to the end of the earth" (49:6). Jesus echoes this: "You are the light of the world" (Matthew 5:14). He tells his followers that their light should not be hidden but put on a stand to give light to others.

A light is not meant to be hidden. It serves no purpose when it is covered up. Rather, a light serves its purpose best when it is put on a stand, lifted up high. That is when it can give light to the greatest number of people.

SLAYING OUR GOLIATHS ———————————————

Has it been working? How are things at The Falls Church Episcopal? Well, the jury is still very much out, and we have a long way to go, but as of this writing, thanks be to God, things look promising.

Since returning to the property, we have seen attendance grow from an average of eighty on a Sunday to just under 250 on a Sunday. That is not explosive growth—we still maintain a sense of community, intimacy, and familiarity—but it is encouraging and sustainable growth. Soon after returning to our property, we scored a major coup in bringing on a dynamic minister of music who provides and oversees a program of vibrant and classical music Sunday by Sunday. With her help, we have launched a popular concert series to benefit local musicians. We brought in an associate for parish life and families to help us not only continue to serve many new families but also to meet our administrative and communications needs. Our day school maintains a waiting list, guaranteeing that the squeals of preschoolers will continue to echo off the walls five days a week. We have almost caught up on years of deferred maintenance, with our administrator overseeing the sprucing up of our hallways with fresh coats of paint and new, helpful signage, as well as the work of many volunteers restoring the historic property and grounds.

We have let the wider community know we are here to serve, and there is hardly ever an evening that our facilities are not in use by some local organization. We transformed what was once a tape library and bookstore into a food pantry and have formed new partnerships with those serving the homeless and prisoners in our area and the poor around the world. We are delighted to welcome newcomers every Sunday. Better yet, most of them not only stay but also throw themselves into the life and ministries of the church, and they are generously supporting its work. In August, 2015, we took a leap of faith and called a new full-time clergy associate to focus on our growing population of middle and high school youth.

All that growth is good, but the most important growth we see is our members' growth in faith, hope, and love. The best and most encouraging growth is when someone is touched by God through their involvement in this church, and that touch makes them more faithful, more hopeful, and more loving in their everyday life.

Challenges remain, of course. Barring a miracle—and I am in the business of believing in miracles, so who knows—it will take several years of sustained growth and continuing generosity from even more people to get us to a point where we are confident about our finances. Relatively speaking, we are still a very small church community in a very large church facility.

But we believe in God, and we believe in each other, and we believe that God has exciting plans for our continued healing and growth. Glory to God, whose power working in us can do infinitely more than we can ask or imagine!

To paraphrase C.S. Lewis, humility is not thinking less of yourself; it is thinking of *yourself, less*. Remember when David encountered the ridicule of his brothers, but he didn't get defensive? He didn't need to defend himself against their accusations because his thoughts were not on himself at all: They were elsewhere, namely, on God's protection and Saul's promises. Remember when King Saul said David was only a boy and inexperienced in battle, but David didn't deny it? He didn't need to deny his weaknesses, because his thoughts were not on himself at all, but on God's strengths.

When David goes running toward Goliath while all the rest of the army runs away from him, David is not thinking less of himself— he knows he is good with a slingshot—but rather he is thinking of himself less and thinking of God more.

That is the difference between self-confidence and God-confidence. Self-confidence is fragile, because anything that makes us think less of ourselves undermines it. God-confidence is solid, because anything that makes us think of ourselves less means more of our mind is free to think about God and others.

David was filled not with self-confidence, but God-confidence. God-confidence means being a light to the nations, the light of the world. What you are good at, God wants to use.

The David and Goliath story therefore ends with David's actions giving courage to the whole army behind him. What he is good at, God uses for the benefit of others.

When you remain focused on God and God's protection, stay confident in God's strength, and slay your seemingly insurmountable problem, keep in mind that others are watching and your actions will give courage to them.

Just like David, your talent, your personality, your God-confidence, your light is lifted up not so people can see it, but so that others are illuminated and encouraged.

FOR FURTHER REFLECTION:

1. Goliath's own weapon becomes his undoing. Other biblical examples of this situation are also provided. Can you think of other times in the Bible and in your own life when a perceived advantage becomes a weakness or liability? What about vice versa, when a perceived weakness or liability turns out to be an advantage?

2. David's deep faith and God-confidence gave him the courage to face the giant Goliath and, against all odds, slay him with a single smooth stone flung from a simple slingshot. Have you ever experienced a faith so deep it emboldened you to face your own giants? How can you develop your own God-confidence? Where will you find your smooth stone?

3. What do you think Archbishop Tutu meant when he said "each one of us is a God-carrier"? Have you ever felt like a God-carrier? When?

AFTERWORD

I hope that you have experienced the David and Goliath story as a story for modern times, modern problems, modern giants. If you previously thought of it as a simple children's story, I hope you now consider it a story that speaks to you as an adult, with all your complex emotional yearnings. I hope you have a deeper appreciation for its nuanced storytelling. I pray it has spoken to you across the centuries.

This ancient story speaks to modern people wrestling with modern issues. God speaks hope to us about timeless issues that we all face at one point or another in life, issues like psychological intimidation and bullying, twisted and broken family dynamics, sibling rivalries, and petty jealousies.

God knows that even the most confident people are subject to horrible insecurities, and so God shows us a way, through David, to handle those who question our abilities. God knows well-intentioned people try to impose their Saul's armor on us, and so God offers a courageous and wise way to reject that armor without rejecting those who offer it, so we can be free to use our God-given gifts.

Most of all, I hope a deep spiritual hunger within you has been fed through this story and through this retelling of it. I hope you have a deeper sense that you are not alone in your struggles, that indeed the same God who cared for David cares for you and will be with you always, even and especially when you face and slay your giants.

I would like to end with a prayer.

Dear God,

When I hear the taunts of my giant, may I remember the dynamics of psychological intimidation, especially the power of words.

When I hear grumbling, when I encounter broken family dynamics and petty jealousies, and my own insecurities are stirred, may I remember David and how he responds to those who challenge his ability to take on his Goliath. May I be reminded whom to put my trust and faith in, and where calm confidence comes from.

When I am offered Saul's armor of ideas, customs, or traditions that don't fit, may I have the courage to reject it without rejecting the Saul who offers it, so I can be free to use my own five smooth stones. And as I slay my Goliath, may I become a light to others.

Most of all, and best of all, may my deepest hunger be satisfied when I remember this sacred story, a story about God and God's care, love and protection for me.

Amen.

The Right Sr Thomas Worshipfull
Bathamptoñ Mompeson of
of Wilts in the County
For ye Advancement of this Knight.
Patronage it is humbly Work. Contributed this Plate, to Whose
dedicated by Richard Blome.

θ Froman delin.   M. vander Gucht Sculp.

85)   *Goliah slaine* —   1. Samuel 17.

ABOUT
THE AUTHOR

John Ohmer has more than twenty years of experience as a parish priest in The Episcopal Church. He joined The Falls Church Episcopal as rector in September, 2012, after having led the growing, vibrant congregation of St. James' Episcopal Church in Leesburg, Virginia for thirteen years. He is a graduate of Wabash College and earned a Master of Divinity from Virginia Theological Seminary. Prior to ordination, he had a brief career in government and politics, working as a Capitol Hill staff member and as a press secretary and speech writer in his home state of Indiana. John and his wife, Mary, an elementary school teacher, have three children. John blogs at Unapologetic Theology, unapologetictheology.blogspot.com.

ABOUT
FORWARD MOVEMENT

Forward Movement is committed to inspiring disciples and empowering evangelists. While we produce great resources like this book, Forward Movement is not a publishing company. We are a ministry.

Our mission is to support you in your spiritual journey, to help you grow as a follower of Jesus Christ. Publishing books, daily reflections, studies for small groups, and online resources is an important way that we live out this ministry. More than a half million people read our daily devotions through *Forward Day by Day*, which is also available in Spanish (*Adelante Día a Día*) and Braille, online, as a podcast, and as an app for your smartphones or tablets. It is mailed to more than fifty countries, and we donate nearly 30,000 copies each quarter to prisons, hospitals, and nursing homes. We actively seek partners across the Church and look for ways to provide resources that inspire and challenge.

A ministry of The Episcopal Church for eighty years, Forward Movement is a nonprofit organization funded by sales of resources and gifts from generous donors. To learn more about Forward Movement and our resources, please visit us at www.forwardmovement.org (or www.adelanteenelcamino.org).

We are delighted to be doing this work and invite your prayers and support.

APPENDIX

1 SAMUEL 17

Now the Philistines gathered their armies for battle; they were gathered at Socoh, which belongs to Judah, and encamped between Socoh and Azekah, in Ephes-dammim. Saul and the Israelites gathered and encamped in the valley of Elah, and formed ranks against the Philistines. The Philistines stood on the mountain on the one side, and Israel stood on the mountain on the other side, with a valley between them. And there came out from the camp of the Philistines a champion named Goliath, of Gath, whose height was six cubits and a span. He had a helmet of bronze on his head, and he was armed with a coat of mail; the weight of the coat was five thousand shekels of bronze. He had greaves of bronze on his legs and a javelin of bronze slung between his shoulders. The shaft of his spear was like a weaver's beam, and his spear's head weighed six hundred shekels of iron; and his shield-bearer went before him. He stood and shouted to the ranks of Israel, "Why have you come out to draw up for battle? Am I not a Philistine, and are you not servants of Saul? Choose a man for yourselves, and let him come down to me. If he is able to fight with me and kill me, then we will be your servants; but if I prevail against him and kill him, then you shall be our servants and serve us." And the Philistine said, "Today I defy the ranks of Israel! Give me a man, that we may fight together." When Saul and all Israel heard these words of the Philistine, they were dismayed and greatly afraid.

Now David was the son of an Ephrathite of Bethlehem in Judah, named Jesse, who had eight sons. In the days of Saul the man was already old and advanced in years. The three eldest sons of Jesse had followed Saul to the battle; the names of his three sons who went to the battle were Eliab the firstborn, and next to him Abinadab, and the third Shammah. David was the youngest; the three eldest followed Saul, but David went back and forth from Saul to feed his father's sheep at Bethlehem. For forty days the Philistine came forward and took his stand, morning and evening.

Jesse said to his son David, "Take for your brothers an ephah of this parched grain and these ten loaves, and carry them quickly to the camp to your brothers; also take these ten cheeses to the commander of their thousand. See how your brothers fare, and bring some token from them."

Now Saul, and they, and all the men of Israel, were in the valley of Elah, fighting with the Philistines. David rose early in the morning, left the sheep with a keeper, took the provisions, and went as Jesse had commanded him. He came to the encampment as the army was going forth to the battle line, shouting the war cry. Israel and the Philistines drew up for battle, army against army. David left the things in charge of the keeper of the baggage, ran to the ranks, and went and greeted his brothers. As he talked with them, the champion, the Philistine of Gath, Goliath by name, came up out of the ranks of the Philistines, and spoke the same words as before. And David heard him.

All the Israelites, when they saw the man, fled from him and were very much afraid. The Israelites said, "Have you seen this man who has come up? Surely he has come up to defy Israel. The king will greatly enrich the man who kills him, and will give him his daughter and make his family free in Israel." David said to the men who stood by him, "What shall be done for the man who kills this Philistine, and takes away the reproach from Israel? For who is this uncircumcised Philistine that he should defy the armies of the living God?" The people answered him in the same way, "So shall it be done for the man who kills him."

His eldest brother Eliab heard him talking to the men; and Eliab's anger was kindled against David. He said, "Why have you come down? With whom have you left those few sheep in the wilderness? I know your presumption and the evil of your heart; for you have come down just to see the battle." David said, "What have I done now? It was only a question." He turned away from him toward another and spoke in the same way; and the people answered him again as before.

When the words that David spoke were heard, they repeated them before Saul; and he sent for him. David said to Saul, "Let no one's heart fail because of him; your servant will go and fight with this Philistine." Saul said to David, "You are not able to go against this Philistine to fight with him; for you are just a boy, and he has been a warrior from his youth." But David said to Saul, "Your servant used to keep sheep for his father; and whenever a lion or a bear came, and took a lamb from the flock, I went after it and struck it down, rescuing the lamb from its mouth; and if it turned against me, I would catch it by the jaw, strike it down, and kill it. Your servant has killed both lions and bears; and this uncircumcised Philistine shall be like one of them, since he has defied the armies of the living God." David said, "The LORD, who saved me from the paw of the lion and from the paw of the bear, will save me from the hand of this Philistine." So Saul said to David, "Go, and may the LORD be with you!"

Saul clothed David with his armor; he put a bronze helmet on his head and clothed him with a coat of mail. David strapped Saul's sword over the armor, and he tried in vain to walk, for he was not used to them. Then David said to Saul, "I cannot walk with these; for I am not used to them." So David removed them.

Then he took his staff in his hand, and chose five smooth stones from the wadi, and put them in his shepherd's bag, in the pouch; his sling was in his hand, and he drew near to the Philistine.

The Philistine came on and drew near to David, with his shield-bearer in front of him. When the Philistine looked and saw David, he disdained him, for he was only a youth, ruddy and handsome in appearance. The Philistine said to David, "Am I a dog, that you come to me with sticks?" And the Philistine cursed David by his gods. The Philistine said to David, "Come to me, and I will give your flesh to the birds of the air and to the wild animals of the field." But David said to the Philistine, "You come to me with sword and spear and javelin; but I come to you in the name of the LORD of hosts, the God of the armies of Israel, whom you have defied. This very day the LORD will deliver you into my hand, and I will strike you down and cut off your head; and I will give the dead bodies of the Philistine army this very day to the birds of the air and to the wild animals of the earth, so that all the earth may know that there is a God in Israel, and that all this assembly may know that the LORD does not save by sword and spear; for the battle is the LORD's and he will give you into our hand."

When the Philistine drew nearer to meet David, David ran quickly toward the battle line to meet the Philistine. David put his hand in his bag, took out a stone, slung it, and struck the Philistine on his forehead; the stone sank into his forehead, and he fell face down on the ground.

So David prevailed over the Philistine with a sling and a stone, striking down the Philistine and killing him; there was no sword in David's hand. Then David ran and stood over the Philistine; he grasped his sword, drew it out of its sheath, and killed him; then he cut off his head with it.

When the Philistines saw that their champion was dead, they fled. The troops of Israel and Judah rose up with a shout and pursued the Philistines as far as Gath and the gates of Ekron, so that the wounded Philistines fell on the way from Shaaraim as far as Gath and Ekron. The Israelites came back from chasing the Philistines, and they plundered their camp. David took the head of the Philistine and brought it to Jerusalem; but he put his armor in his tent.

When Saul saw David go out against the Philistine, he said to Abner, the commander of the army, "Abner, whose son is this young man?" Abner said, "As your soul lives, O king, I do not know." The king said, "Inquire whose son the stripling is." On David's return from killing the Philistine, Abner took him and brought him before Saul, with the head of the Philistine in his hand. Saul said to him, "Whose son are you, young man?" And David answered, "I am the son of your servant Jesse the Bethlehemite."

GOLIATHS IN OUR LAND

Here are some examples of present-day Goliaths.

Personal	Congregational/ vocational/ professional/ ministerial	Spiritual: the principalities and powers/spirits set against us
Caregiver burden	Dualistic thinking or knowing	Spirit of self-righteous superiority
Health issues		
Time management	Preference for fellowship over discipleship	Negativity/claim of hypocrisy
Insecurity	How to be loving and accessible when facing resistance to change	Greed of international corporations
Financial		
Organizational skills		Fundamentalism
Perfectionism	Money vs. aging infrastructure	Neurotic need for certainty
Energy	Growth difficult in a small town struggling economically	Out of date language
Threat of lawsuit		
Myself: not good enough	Congregation too small	Image of "liberal" church
Too many ideas, too little energy	Apathy	Christians no longer trustworthy in our story and in our behavior
Career stalemate	Attitude of scarcity	Polarization in church, politics, society
Kids moving away	People who are set in their ways	
Consuming kid problems	Deep conviction of keeping "their church" they way they want it	Fearful of "next" issue to disrupt local congregation
Stress of life changes		
Disorganization	Rich bullies	Blaming
Harmful habits	Building maintenance	Anger
Distractions	Balance spiritual, outreach, and worship	Judgment
Drug problems		Progressive-ism
Being an introvert	Reaching the disillusioned	Racism
Financial limitations		Financial downturn

Relocation	Rebuilding a parish torn by schism	We don't speak in a language the world can hear
Exhaustion		
Weariness	Building up music and Christian formation	Greed
Self criticism	Missing sheep	Poverty and income distribution
Polarization of Christian faith communities	Transition due to age and health	Lack of education
	Privileged community: served rather than serve	Conflicts, war
		Inequality
	Low sense of vocation	Putting people in prison rather than presenting paths of healing and reform
	Complacency	
	Limited resources	
	Lack of enthusiasm	Divisive vs. unifying
	Difficult history	Lack of sense of Christian identity
	Aging demographics	

THE SIX VISIONS OF
THE FALLS CHURCH EPISCOPAL

✔ With God's help, The Falls Church Episcopal will grow both numerically and spiritually: we will draw increasing numbers of newcomers, and invite them into deeper involvement in the ministries of the church while equipping all our members to grow as disciples of Jesus.

> **WHY:** "Do not forget to show hospitality to strangers, for by so doing some people have shown hospitality to angels without knowing it." (Hebrews 13:2)
>
> We are a welcoming group of believers. We are proud of our heritage as Christians worshiping in the Episcopal tradition; we have love for one another, and are an open, outreach-oriented people who offer a sense of community to people seeking connection, purpose, and Christian community. Jesus told his followers that they are "the light of the world;" that "a town built on a hill cannot be hidden," and that we are to "let our light shine before others" so that God may be glorified. We have a "message of trust in the hope-filled promises of Jesus"—in other words, we are, and we have, good news to offer, and we seek to draw others into that good news as we grow in our own discipleship.

✔ With God's help, The Falls Church will encourage and equip all parishioners to live out their baptismal covenant promise to strive for justice and peace among all people, and respect the dignity of every human being.

Why: "What does the Lord require of you but to do justice, and to love kindness, and to walk humbly with your God?" (Micah 6:8).

When Jesus summarized his own "mission," he said he was sent to "to preach good news to the poor, proclaim freedom for the prisoners, recovery of sight for the blind, to release the oppressed, and to proclaim the year of the Lord's favor." As Jesus' followers, we are called not only to address the practical everyday needs of the poor, but in addition, we are each challenged, in our baptismal covenant, to address underlying causes of poverty and injustice.

✔ With God's help, we will provide quality, proactive pastoral care to our members.

> **Why:** "A new command I give you: Love one another. As I have loved you, so you must love one another. By this everyone will know that you are my disciples, if you love one another" (John 13:34-35).
>
> This vision is already taking new wings, with the reactivation of a Stephen Ministry program, and adding staff. This frees the clergy staff to provide pastoral care to those in need, as well as to equip lay leaders who have this gift to share it with others.

✔ With God's help, The Falls Church Episcopal will have a vibrant children and youth ministry.

> **Why:** "Love the LORD your God with all your heart and with all your soul and with all your strength. These commandments that I give you today are to be on your

hearts. Impress them on your children. Talk about them
when you sit at home and when you walk along the road,
when you lie down and when you get up" (Deuteronomy
6:5-6).

Children and youth are not just the future of the church:
They are the church. God seems to be drawing increasing
numbers of families with young children to our worship
services. We rejoice as children find leadership roles in
worship and ministry at The Falls Church. We teach,
through conscious words, programs, and example, the vital
truths of our faith as we prepare children and youth for
lives of Christian leadership and service in the world.
Our vision is to offer a ministry that will attract youth
of the community to our parish because of the quality
of our offerings.

✔ With God's help, The Falls Church will be known for its
outstanding music programs. They will draw children from
disadvantaged backgrounds into affordable or free music
lessons, train a generation of church youth in highest quality
Christian music, and continue to provide church worship
services with vibrant, inspiring vocal and instrumental music.

> WHY: "Sing to the LORD a new song; sing to the LORD,
> all the earth....Declare his glory among the nations, his
> marvelous deeds among all peoples" (Psalm 96).

> Voices and instruments joined in praising God are an
> outward and visible—or at least audible—sign of God's
> kingdom coming, and God's will being done, on earth
> as it is in heaven. They offer a powerful way to worship
> God, creating harmony and beauty as a manifestation of

Christ and the church. Excellent music draws people to the community. Music education offers youth and adults the opportunity to become excellent musicians, trained in traditional and contemporary offerings. The vision of offering voice and instrumental lessons to children of the community with limited financial resources and have them share in the worship of the church is a powerful way to bring good news, with the potential to transform lives.

✔ With God's help, the buildings and grounds of The Falls Church Episcopal—including our adjacent property—will be good news to the community of the city of Falls Church.

> **WHY:** "Unless the LORD builds the house, the builders labor in vain" (Psalm 127:1).

> We believe it is strategically wise to build on our assets, and one of our assets is our buildings and grounds. They are centrally located, historically significant, and spacious. We have an opportunity to offer our buildings and grounds as a tangible way to serve the wider community of Falls Church. We want not only ourselves, but also the place itself—the buildings and grounds— to be known in the wider community as good news, a helpful, open, friendly resource for the betterment of the city. In addition, we have a responsibility to our city, state, and indeed the nation to share our historic building, grounds, artifacts, and historical records with all who want to understand the history of the Episcopal Church in the context of our nation's founding and growth. Further, we wish to offer our facilities to the diocese and to other compatible faith communities and organizations as partners in the gospel.